THE
traditional
AGA
Party BOOK

First published in 1995 by Absolute Press, Scarborough House,
29 James Street West, Bath, BA1 2BT. Tel: 01225 316013 Fax: 01225 445836
Email: sales@absolutepress.demon.co.uk

Reprinted December 1995
Reprinted October 1996
Reprinted October 1997
Reprinted 1998 (twice)

ISBN 0 948230 91 6

Cover and text Design by Ian Middleton
Cover and text illustrations by Caroline Nisbett

Printed by The Cromwell Press, Trowbridge, Wiltshire
Covers printed by Devenish and Co. Bath

THE
traditional
AGA
Party BOOK

Louise Walker

ABSOLUTE PRESS

CONTENTS

GENERAL
INTRODUCTION

CONVERSION CHART

This is the metric/imperial conversion chart that I have used. Do keep to either metric or imperial measures throughout the whole recipe. Mixing the two can lead to all kinds of problems. Eggs used in testing have been size 3. "Tablespoon" and "teaspoon" measures have been flat unless otherwise stated.

Ingredients   Conversion

Ingredients	Conversion
1 oz	25g
2 oz	50g
3 oz	75g
4 oz	100g
5 oz	150g
6 oz	175g
7 oz	200g
8 oz	225g
9 oz	250g
10 oz	275g
11 oz	300g
12 oz	350g
13 oz	375g
14 oz	400g
15 oz	425g
16 oz (1 lb)	450g
1 tsp	5ml
1 tbsp	15ml
1/4 pint	150ml
1/2 pint	300ml
3/4 pint	450ml
1 pint	600ml
8 inch tin	20cm tin

INTRODUCTION

All the Aga owners that I have ever met are keen on party giving, even if they are not enthusiastic cooks. This book is written to give ideas for different festive events around which we create parties, and to give those owners who need it some confidence in planning and preparing for parties and entertaining. If you are completely new to cooking with an Aga, try to spend some time becoming familiar with the techniques needed before launching into entertaining. For this, read the *Traditional Aga Cookery Book*.

Cooking for parties needs to be planned so that all that stored heat in the Aga is not used up before serving time. This is why a few basic principles and techniques should be learnt. Cook everything possible in the ovens to conserve heat – remember that heat loss is greatest when the lids are up. Frying pans can be put on the floor of the roasting oven to sauté and fry food – leave the oven door open slightly if you need to watch the food. Steaming should always be done in the simmering oven once the food is hot through from the top of the Aga. Grill in the top of the roasting oven, and remember that a grilled breakfast is healthier than a fried one! Root vegetables, rice and pasta, once started on the top, can be cooked in the simmering oven. Milk can be warmed, chocolate and butter melted and jams softened just by standing them on top of the Aga, or, if you're in a hurry, in the simmering oven.

The Aga is perfect for cooking for a crowd because the ovens are so large. The large roasting tins can be used for roasting, cooking fish or meat portions in quantity, for baking cakes and puddings. Do not leave any acidic food in the tins too long, however, and transfer to serving dishes when cooked. To save on washing-up, line with foil like Bake-o-Glide. The cold shelf makes a useful baking tray for cooking large items, such as Pavlovas and meringue desserts. I find two cold shelves useful, one to diffuse heat as a cold shelf and one to cook on. If you frequently cook for a lot of people, a large saucepan/casserole is useful. Choose one with oven-proof handles so that it will go on the hob and in the oven. This can be used for cooking pasta, making stock in or even small quantities of jam as well.

Serving plates can be warmed on top of the Aga or in the simmering oven – of course the four-oven Aga has a warming oven for this purpose. Sauces can also be made in advance and kept warm: a little damp grease-proof paper on top, or even cling film, will prevent a skin forming.

PARTY PLANNING

I am the sort of hostess who likes to spend time with her guests and not in the kitchen, so I try to do as much preparation as possible beforehand. This includes laying tables, putting out drinks and glasses, having vegetables prepared and, where possible, one or two courses to serve cold and thus made in advance.

For entertaining, Agas and freezers go well together, so for a large crowd and for an important occasion make some dishes ahead of time and freeze, then thaw and if necessary refresh them in the Aga before serving. Again, when entertaining a large crowd, a little extra help can be useful. Sixth-formers are always glad of a few extra pounds and will help serve the food, clear the table, keep an eye on cooking last-minute vegetables etc. In Bath, where I live, we can hire all cutlery and crockery and then return it unwashed – a boon when you have 20 or more guests.

Throughout the book the recipes have been put into sections, but these are ideas to be swapped around. I have also given smaller quantities for most recipes, e.g. for 6 or 8, but all recipes chosen can be increased easily. For example, make two or three puddings or cook twice as much casserole. Plan the menus for a variety of textures, colour, hot and cold, advanced and last-minute preparation.

QUANTITIES

Most people cook for four to six people daily, so I have given below a few ideas on quantities for parties. If you are serving a selection of main course dishes and puddings, you can usually expect a recipe for 6 to serve 8-9. For a large party it is a good idea to have someone serve the main course food; this helps portion control and means there will be some left for late-comers or the hostess. Keep some good bread in the kitchen to eke out the food if it is going too quickly. Cut puddings into portions beforehand if possible. This is best done when the pudding, if cold, is well chilled.

Remember to keep food covered until it is ready to serve, because the surface will dry out and look stale.

QUANTITIES

Pate	for 1	1½ oz/35g
	for 12	1¼ lbs/600g
Smoked Salmon	for 1	1½ oz/35g
	for 12	1¼ lbs/600g
Soup	for 1	⅓ pint/200ml
	for 12	4 pints/2.5l
Chicken	1 portion per person	8 oz/250g
	or for 12	6½ lbs/3kg whole
		oven ready bird
Turkey	for 12	8 lbs/3.5kg
Meat off bone	1 portion	4 oz/100g
	12 portions	3 lbs/1.5kg
Meat on bone	1 portion	6 oz/175g
	12 portions	4½ lbs/2.5kg
Cold Meats	1 portion	3 oz/75g
	12 portions	2¼ lbs/1.1kg
(Potatoes, Peas,	1 portion	4 oz/100g
Beans, Corn) etc	12 portions	3 lbs/1.5kg
Rice & Pasta	1 portion	1½ oz/35g
(uncooked)	12 portions	1¼ lbs/1.1kg
Cheese	per person	3 oz/75g
Gravy	for 12	1½ pints/900ml
Mayonnaise	for 12	1 pint/600ml
French Dressing	for 12	½ pint/300ml
Cream	for 12	1½ pints/900ml
Brown Bread & Butter	1½ slices per person	
French Bread	1 large loaf cuts into 15 slices	
Biscuits for cheese	allow 2-3 per person	
Butter	allow 1½ oz/35g per person	

DRINKS

Coffee	12 teacups or 25 demi-tasse	4 oz/100g ground coffee, 3 pints/1.7l water
Tea	for 12 (teacups)	1 oz/25g tea, 4 pints/2.3l water and 1½ pints/900ml milk
Cocktails	10-15 mouthfuls per person or 4-5 mouthfuls per person if at pre-dinner drinks	

B A S I C   A G A
T E C H N I Q U E S

F I S H

Cooking fish in the Aga is so easy and cuts out fishy smells. The variety of fish available is increasing all the time, so experiment with different fish and different cooking methods. I have given approximate cooking times, but this will depend upon the size and thickness of the fish. Try not to overcook as this gives dry, stringy, tasteless fish.

P O A C H I N G   F I S H

Place the fish in the roasting tin, cover with water, wine or milk, salt, pepper and a bayleaf. Cover it loosely with foil and hang the tin on the third set of runners from the top for 15-20 minutes.

P O A C H I N G   W H O L E   L A R G E   F I S H   e . g .   S A L M O N

Clean the fish. Sprinkle with salt if desired and wrap in buttered foil. Lift the parcel into the large roasting tin, pour boiling water into the tin to come half-way up the fish. Hang on the second set of runners from the top of the roasting oven. Cook for 10 minutes per lb/450g, turning the fish half-way through cooking. Remove it from the oven and allow to cool. Serve warm or remove skin when cold.

F R I E D   F I S H

Wash and dry the fish. If liked coat with either seasoned flour, batter, oatmeal or egg and fresh breadcrumbs. Put enough cooking oil into the roasting tin to coat the base. Put the tin on the floor of the roasting oven and heat until hazing. Add the fish and continue to cook on the floor of

the oven. Turn the fish half-way through the cooking time.

GRILLED FISH

Lay fish cutlets in a roasting tin, brush with oil and seasoning. Hang the tin on the highest set of runners and grill, turning over half-way through the cooking time. You can ring the changes by marinading the fish for half an hour and grilling on the rack of the roasting tin, basting or brushing with a little more marinade part way through cooking. This will give a more charred appearance and taste.

MEAT

ROASTING MEAT

Meat roasted in the Aga will be moist and flavoursome with only a smearing of extra fat needed to start the cooking. Season as you prefer: salt, pepper, fresh herbs etc. If the meat is to be stuffed, do this and then weigh it to calculate cooking times. There are two methods of roasting using the Aga. The Quick Roasting Method is the more traditional method, used for more tender cuts of meat. The Slow Roasting Method is best for less fine cuts of meat.

QUICK ROASTING METHOD

Season the meat and put in the Aga roasting tin. Stand it on the rack if you prefer. Hang the tin on the bottom set of runners of the roasting oven for the calculated time and baste periodically with hot fat. The shape of the joint will also affect the cooking time — a long narrow joint will not take so long as a short, fat joint. When the meat is cooked, allow the joint to rest in the simmering oven for 15 minutes before carving. This is a useful time to make gravy and cook last-minute vegetables.

SLOW ROASTING METHOD

Season and prepare the meat as above. Put the roasting tin into the roasting oven on the bottom set of runners for 30 minutes or until the meat is browning and getting hot. Transfer to the bottom set of runners of the simmering oven and cook for twice the time calculated for the quick roasting method.

TIMES FOR ROASTING:

Roast Beef :

rare	10 minutes per lb/450g plus 10 minutes
medium	15 minutes per lb/450g plus 15 minutes
well done	20 minutes per lb/450g plus 20 minutes
fillet	10 minutes per lb/450g plus 10 minutes

Roast Pork:

30 minutes per lb/450g plus 30 minutes

Lamb:

pink	15 minutes per lb/450g plus 15 minutes
medium	20 minutes per lb/450g plus 20 minutes

Veal:

20 minutes per lb/450g plus 20 minutes

ROASTING POULTRY AND GAME

Roast poultry and game from the Aga will be crisp-skinned on the outside with moist, tender flesh. Most poultry is cooked in the roasting oven by the normal method, but a large turkey can be cooked in the simmering oven, useful when cooking for a crowd or to take the rush and bustle from Christmas morning. Nowadays it is not considered safe to stuff

poultry before roasting, though the neck end of turkey can still be filled if not the cavity. Always allow extra cooking time for this stuffing. Smear the bird with a little butter. Put bacon rashers over the breast if required and stand it on the trivet in the roasting tin. Put lemon or herbs in the body cavity if liked. Cover with a little foil – wrapping it tightly will slow the cooking time. Hang the tin on the lowest set of runners for the following times. Remove the foil for the last $\frac{1}{4}$ hour to allow browning.

ROASTING TIMES

(N.B: ensure that oven is up to correct temperature before roasting.)

Bird	Weight	Approximate cooking times
Chicken	2lb/1kg	45-50 minutes
	3lb/1.5kg	1 hour
	4lb/2kg	$1\frac{1}{2}$ hours
	5lb/2.5kg	$1\frac{3}{4}$ hours
Turkey	Weigh the bird after stuffing and allow 15 minutes per 450g/1lb + 15 minutes. Remove from oven and leave for 30 minutes to allow the flesh to firm up.	
Duck		1-$1\frac{1}{2}$ hours
Goose		$1\frac{1}{2}$-2 hours
Grouse		30-35 minutes
Pigeon		20-35 minutes
Partridge		30-35 minutes
Pheasant		45-50 minutes
Quail		15 minutes
Snipe		15 minutes
Woodcock		15 minutes

To test if cooked, pierce the thickest part of the thigh with a fine skewer, and if the juices run clear the bird is cooked. Allow the bird to rest in the simmering oven whilst making gravy from the skimmed cooking juices.

SLOW ROASTING OF TURKEY

Prepare the turkey in the usual way and stand it on the rack in the roasting tin. Cover loosely with foil and slide onto the floor of the simmering oven for the following length of time:

8-10lb/4-5kg	about 9-10 hours
11-15lb/5.5-7.5kg	about 11-12 hours
16-22lb/8-11kg	about 13-14 hours

Remove the foil and pop the turkey into the roasting oven for the last 15 minutes of cooking time to crisp the skin. Test in the usual way.

B O I L E D   B A C O N   A N D   G A M M O N   J O I N T S

Cooking a whole piece of ham in the Aga is so easy and gives a moist joint, perfect for slicing. I even cook ham for friends because they love the moistness, and really it takes very little effort.

Soak the joint in water for 2-3 hours to remove any saltiness. Put a trivet or an old saucer in the bottom of a suitably sized pan. Put the joint on top and pour in enough cold water to come 2-3 inches up the side of the pan. Cover. Stand the pan on the simmering plate and bring slowly to the boil, simmering for 30 minutes. Transfer to the floor of the simmering oven for the following times:

2-3 lb/1-1.5kg	2½ hours
4-5 lb/2-2.5kg	3 hours
6-7 lb/3-3.5kg	3½ hours
8-9 lb/4-4.5kg	4½ hours
10-11 lb/5-5.5kg	5½ hours
12-13 lb/6-6.5kg	6½ hours
14-15 lb/7-7.5kg	7½ hours
16 lb/7.5kg and over	overnight

Remove the pan from the oven and the ham from the pan and allow it to cool a little, to handle. Strip off the skin and score the fat. Mix together a glaze of mustard and honey and spread over the surface. Stud with cloves. Stand the ham in a roasting tin with the glazing uppermost and cover the meat with foil. Hang the tin so that the meat is fairly near the top of the roasting oven and bake for 10-20 minutes until a golden glaze has formed. Watch it closely, it may burn. Serve hot or cold.

STOCKS

....

Home-made stocks are easy to make in the Aga and they certainly taste better than stock cubes. If you make a large potful, freeze in quantities that are most useful: 1 pint/600ml for soups, ½ pint/300ml for gravies etc.

BEEF, LAMB, CHICKEN, GAME ETC.

....

Place the bones of the chosen meat in a large saucepan. Add a selection of flavouring vegetables e.g. onions, carrots, celery, washed and chopped, but not necessarily peeled. Add some peppercorns and a bouquet garni. Cover with cold water and put on a lid. Place on the boiling plate and bring to the boil. Transfer to the simmering plate and simmer for 10 minutes. Transfer to the simmering oven and leave for 12 hours or overnight. Remove the saucepan from the oven, cool and skim off excess fat. Strain through a sieve and either store in the fridge for immediate use, or freeze it. For a darker stock, roast the bones in a roasting tin on the bottom set of runners of the roasting oven for 45 minutes before proceeding as above.

VEGETABLE STOCK

....

Wash and chop a selection of vegetables, for example onions, carrots, leeks, celery, turnips, broccoli. Place them in a large pan and cover with water. Add a few peppercorns and a bouquet garni of whatever fresh herbs are to hand. Bring to the boil on the boiling plate, move to the simmering plate and simmer for 10 minutes. Transfer to the simmering oven and leave for 3-4 hours. Remove and strain through a sieve. Discard the now flavourless vegetables. Pack and freeze the cold stock or store in the fridge for immediate use.

FISH STOCK

....

Take a selection of bones from unsmoked fish and place in a saucepan. Add washed and roughly chopped vegetables like carrots and onions, a few peppercorns and a bouquet garni. Cover with fresh, cold water. Bring

to the boil on the boiling plate, move to the simmering plate and simmer for 10 minutes. Transfer to the simmering oven and cook for 1 hour. Remove from the oven, strain through a sieve and store the cold stock in the fridge for 2 days or in the freezer for no more than 2 months.

BOILED POTATOES AND OTHER ROOT VEGETABLES

Potatoes, along with other root vegetables, are best cooked in the simmering oven. This both conserves the stored heat in the Aga and prevents the kitchen filling with steam. You will need to use a pan that can be used on the boiling plate and in the simmering oven, so avoid wooden handles. Do not be tempted to transfer the potatoes to a cold serving dish part of the way through cooking – the entire heat of the pan, water and vegetables is needed for successful cooking.

Wash and prepare the potatoes in the usual way. Cut them to an even size. Place in the pan, add salt to taste, and cover with cold water. Put on the lid and bring to the boil on the boiling plate. When boiling well, pour off the water and transfer to the simmering oven. It is difficult to give timings, as the length of cooking time will depend upon the type of potato and the size of them. Allow 30 minutes and then test. Small new potatoes and small pieces of root vegetable will take about 20 minutes. Drain the vegetables, toss in butter if liked, and serve or return to the pan and the oven to keep warm.

ROASTING VEGETABLES

Roast vegetables are always a great favourite. I know that it is fashionably healthy to eat baked potatoes instead of roast, and steamed instead of roast parsnips, but nothing beats roast vegetables with roast meat for a special treat. Peel and cut the vegetables to an even size. Boil for one minute in salted water, then drain thoroughly. While the vegetables are draining and drying, put some cooking oil, lard or dripping into the roasting tin. Slide into the roasting oven on the second set of runners from the top. When the fat is hot, tip in the dry vegetables, toss them in the fat and return to the oven. If you are also roasting meat it may be

necessary to juggle the tins during cooking. Cooking near the top will give an evenly cooked, crispy vegetable. Putting the tin on the floor of the oven will crisp the bottom of the vegetables well. They can be put into the top of the baking oven in the 4-oven Aga but they may need to be finally crisped in the top of the roasting oven. Vegetables take about 1 hour to roast. If the vegetables are put around the meat they may take longer and are often not so crispy, but they do taste wonderful!

COOKING RICE

A lot of people seem to have trouble cooking rice. Cooked in the simmering oven of the Aga, it is very simple, and it can be kept hot without spoiling if you want to cook it slightly in advance. This is the basic method for cooking rice. Adjust the quantities to suit your needs. Use a pan that will transfer from the boiling plate to the simmering oven.

1 cup rice
1 1/2 cups water
good pinch salt

Wash the rice in a sieve with cold, running water and put it in the saucepan. Add salt and water and put on the lid. Bring to the boil on the boiling plate. When boiling, transfer the pan to the floor of the simmering oven. Cook for the appropriate time. The times I have given produce a cooked, non-soggy rice. If you like rice a little more cooked, then leave it in the oven a little longer. Remove from the oven and drain through a sieve – some rice will have absorbed all the water. Rinse with boiling water and serve. Alternatively, if you want to keep the rice hot, return it to the pan and stir in a small knob of butter. Cover and return to the simmering oven until required.

COOKING TIMES:

White long-grain rice	12 minutes
Brown long-grain rice	20 minutes
Basmati rice	12 minutes

COOKING PASTA

Pasta needs a fast boil when cooking, to prevent it sticking together. Try to use a pan that is deeper than its width. Half fill with water, add salt to taste, put the lid on and bring to the boil on the boiling plate. Add the pasta, fresh or dried, cover and bring back to the boil – this will not take long. Remove the lid and start timing according to the packet instructions. It may be necessary to move the pan half-on, half-off the boiling plate to prevent the water boiling over, but try to keep the water and pasta moving. When *al dente*, drain through a colander, return to the pan and toss in a little oil or butter to prevent sticking. Serve straight away with a chosen sauce.

DRIED BEANS AND PEAS

The range of dried beans available in the shops gives a whole host of flavours, colours and textures for cooking. The beans and other grains can be used for vegetarian cooking or to make meat dishes go further, or just to add variety. Lentils do not need soaking before cooking, just washing and picking over. All the other pulses need to be washed, picked over and left to soak for 8-12 hours or overnight, so some forethought is necessary.

Measure out the pulses required, wash well and pick over to remove any grit. Place in a bowl and cover with cold water. Put aside to soak. Drain the liquid from the beans. Place them in a saucepan, cover with cold water and bring to the boil. Boil rapidly for 10 minutes – to prevent the water from boiling over, use a large pan and no lid at this stage. After 10 minutes' rapid boil, cover and transfer to the simmering oven until tender, 1-3 hours. The length of time depends upon the type and age of the bean. Experience will be your best judge. When cooked, use as per recipe.

CAKES

During my Aga demonstrations I have heard so many people say, 'I am told you cannot make a cake in an Aga.' Nothing could be further from the truth, it is just a matter of knowing HOW to make a cake in an Aga.

The 4-oven Aga has a special baking oven, so cake-making is easy. Just use that oven for all cakes, unless you wish to cook a rich fruit cake overnight in the simmering oven. The 2-oven Aga has a very hot roasting oven, which may seem too hot for cooking at lower temperatures.

Each Aga should have a large plain baking sheet, made of aluminium, known as the cold plain shelf. Cold is the most important word here. Store this shelf, not in the oven, but in a cool cupboard. The cold shelf is put in above cakes or biscuits to reduce the top heat and allow the cake to cook through without burning. Always allow rising space and air circulation space – usually 2 runners above the oven shelf. If you are doing a large baking session, take the shelf out periodically to allow it to cool down and therefore become effective again. The cold plain shelf can be used as an oven shelf, and food such as scones can, of course, be put above it when it is being used as a cold shelf.

The other option for making deeper cakes that take several hours to bake is the Aga cake baker. The empty cake baker is heated up in the roasting oven while the cake is being made. The mixture is put into one of the tins provided, which is then put in the trivet and the whole thing put into the hot, empty cake baker. This is returned to the roasting oven and the cake cooked for the required time. The cake baker insulates the cake, allowing it to cook through without burning. If converting a recipe, check the cake during cooking as the final baking time may be shorter.

BREAD AND YEAST COOKERY

Bread and yeast-based dishes are so easy and successful using the Aga, not just because the roasting oven is so good for baking bread, but because the steady heat is perfect for warming and rising the bread dough. For a quick bread mix and for a store-cupboard standby, the easy-blend yeast in measured sachets is easy to use, and quick. However, if you have time, try using fresh yeast and let the dough rise twice, for a fuller flavour and better texture. Fresh yeast can be bought from health food shops, bakers and the fresh-bake counters in supermarkets. Store it in a plastic box in the fridge for about 10 days; should it go runny or smell rancid, throw it away and start with new yeast.

The choice of flour is largely personal. Organic flour comes in brown and white for bread-making, or standard strong white or brown can be used, or a mixture of both. Special flours such as rye or granary may be found at more specialist food shops. The quantities of liquids given in the recipes can only be guidelines, because all flours vary in the amount of liquid they absorb. Try to make the dough as moist as possible, without being too sticky to handle, as this will give a better finished product. The main problem with bread-making is trying not to kill the yeast. I warm the liquid by standing it on top of the Aga, so that it will be at blood heat and no hotter – it should be warm to the touch only. If the liquid is too hot, the yeast will be killed before it can do its work. I have given a few basic recipes, but once you have mastered the art of bread-making, you can enjoy trying out new ideas and new recipes from other books.

CHRISTMAS

Christmas is the season of entertaining family and friends, and the day itself should be relaxing and enjoyable. The secret to all entertaining is planning ahead. But do not carry planning in advance too far, after all, you don't want to be exhausted before the feasting begins! I try to make my cakes and puddings in October, because they really do improve with keeping. However, we all have years when planning goes out of the window, so there are recipes for last-minute cakes and puddings too. Mincemeats also benefit for keeping and will not ferment if heated slowly in the simmering oven before putting into jars.

Few houses have cold pantries these days, so I usually wrap my cakes and puddings and freeze them, but of course, rich fruit cakes and puddings will keep in a cool cupboard – the Aga kitchen is far too warm.

Towards the end of November some pre-preparation can take place, for example, a few main courses and puddings can be made and frozen in the weeks before Christmas. Make some interesting breads which can be defrosted for a quick ploughman's lunch with good cheese, cold meat and home-made pickles. Chutneys and relishes benefit from storing for at least 4 weeks, so prepare these in advance, making a couple of extra jars for presents. I also try to make sauces and stuffings early in December and freeze them, e.g. cranberry sauce, bread sauce, brandy butter.

If you have room in your freezer, some special sponge cakes can be made, decorated and frozen on baking sheets. When frozen hard, wrap them well and store carefully. To thaw, unwrap the cakes, stand them on a serving plate and allow to thaw slowly. A lot of nibbles can be made in advance and 'refreshed' for a few minutes in the roasting or baking oven.

On Christmas Eve I try to do a little pre-preparation so that there is time to watch the children unwrap presents and play with their toys before Christmas dinner. Remember to give the Aga a boost of extra heat the night before. Peel potatoes and other root vegetables, par-boil and toss them in oil ready for roasting the next day. The pudding only needs an hour of steaming, but it certainly will not harm if you want to put it in to steam 2-3 hours in advance – follow the recipe instructions. Sauces can be made on the day and kept warm either in the simmering oven or on top of the Aga or made the day before and re-heated just before serving.

RICH CHRISTMAS CAKE

Rich fruit cakes baked in the simmering oven are beautifully moist, evenly cooked and level. However, the timing may vary according to your simmering oven. Some are 'hot' and the cake may cook in 4 hours, even with a piece of foil on the top to prevent browning, or if 'cool' the cake may be fine in the oven for 12 hours or more. The timing I give is for a gas, two-oven Aga.

8 oz/225g butter, warm and soft
8 oz/225g soft brown sugar
8 oz/225g plain flour
1 level tsp ground mixed spice
1 level tsp ground cinnamon
1/2 level tsp ground ginger
1/2 level tsp ground nutmeg
1/2 level tsp bicarbonate of soda
1/2 level tsp salt
1 apple, cored, peeled and grated
grated rind of 1 orange
4 eggs, beaten
10 oz/275g currants
10 oz/275g sultanas
10 oz/275g raisins
4 oz/100g glacé cherries, halved and washed
2 oz/50g slivered almonds
1 tbsp black treacle
5 tbsp brandy
Greased and lined 8"/20cm round and deep cake tin.

Cream together the butter and sugar. Sieve the flour together with the remaining dry ingredients. Beat the eggs, about 1 at a time, into the butter mixture, adding 1 tsp flour mixture with each addition to prevent curdling. When all the egg is used up, add the treacle, grated apple and orange rind. Mix well. Fold in the fruit, nuts and remaining flour and finally the brandy. Stir well.

Spoon into the prepared tin, and level the top. Bake for approximately 8 hours, depending upon the temperature of the simmering oven, until the cake looks 'dry' on the top and a skewer inserted into the middle comes out clean. Cool in the tin. When the cake is cold, either wrap it in foil or place it in an airtight tin in a cool place until ready to marzipan and ice.

LEAMINGTON FESTIVAL CAKE

I have no idea where the name for this cake came from. We always made this as the Christmas cake at college in Gloucester, and it has become a family favourite since. The quantities make one 8"/20cm cake.

2 oranges, grated rind and juice
3 oz/75ml brandy
4 oz/100g glacé cherries, halved and washed
10 oz/275g raisins
12 oz/350g sultanas
8 oz/225g currants
2 oz/50g chopped almonds, toasted
8 oz/225g butter, softened
6 oz/175g demerara sugar
4 eggs, beaten
6 oz/175g self-raising flour
4 oz/100g plain flour
pinch salt
2 oz/50g ground almonds
2 heaped tsp ground mixed spice
2 tbsp black treacle
2 tbsp golden syrup
2 fl oz/50ml milk

The day before making, mix together the orange rind and juice, brandy, cherries, raisins, sultanas and currants. Cover and leave to soak overnight.

Cream together the sugar and butter until light and fluffy. Sieve together the flours, salt and mixed spice. Beat in the eggs, one at a time, with 1 tsp flour, to the butter mixture. Fold in the remaining flour mixture and ground almonds. Add the toasted chopped nuts and soaked fruit. Mix the treacle, golden syrup and milk together and stir into the cake mixture. Stir well. When thoroughly mixed, pour into a greased and lined 8"/20cm deep round cake tin. To bake in the two-oven Aga put the oven shelf on the floor of the roasting oven, put in the cake and slide the cold shelf two sets of runners above the top of the cake tin. Cook for 20-30 minutes – do not allow to over-brown. Transfer to the simmering oven for 6-8 hours, depending upon the heat of the oven. Cooler ovens may need overnight cooking. For the four-oven Aga, put the oven shelf on the floor of the baking oven, put in the cake and bake for 30 minutes. Transfer to the simmering oven and bake as above. The cake is cooked when a warm skewer inserted into the middle of the cake comes out clean. Cool in the tin. Decorate with marzipan, icing or as liked.

ALMOND FUDGE CAKE

A cake for nut lovers! With the almond paste in the middle and a fudge topping, this makes a delicious 'special-occasion' cake.

4 oz/100g whole almonds
4 oz/100g almond paste
6 oz/175g butter or margarine
6 oz/175g caster sugar
1 tsp vanilla essence
3 eggs
8 oz/225g self-raising flour
1 tsp ground cinnamon
1-2 tbsp milk

TOPPING
2 oz/50g butter or margarine
4 oz/100g soft brown sugar
1 tbsp double cream

For the two-oven Aga, put the cake baker to heat in the roasting oven. Base-line and grease a 7"/18cm round cake tin. Shred the skinned almonds and toast them on a baking tray towards the top of the roasting oven. WATCH them, as they burn easily! Roll the almond paste to a 7"/18cm circle. Set aside. Beat together the butter, sugar, vanilla essence, beaten eggs, flour and cinnamon until the mixture is light, fluffy and well mixed. Fold in $3/_4$ of the nuts and enough milk to make a soft dropping consistency. Spoon half the cake mixture into the prepared tin. Place the circle of almond paste on top. Cover with remaining cake mixture. Level the surface.

For the two-oven Aga, place the tin in the pre-heated cake baker and bake for one hour. For the four-oven Aga, put the shelf on the floor of the baking oven and bake the cake for $1-1^1/_2$ hours. Bake until the cake is risen, golden and firm to the touch. Cool in the tin for 5 minutes before turning out onto a cooling rack. Stand the cooled cake, still on the rack, over a baking tray or plate. For the topping, place the butter, sugar and cream in a saucepan. Stand the pan on the simmering plate and stir until blended and the butter has melted. Bring to the boil. Remove from the heat and stir in the remaining almonds. Pour over the cake. Allow to cool and set for 5-10 minutes.

Serves 10-12.

BUCHE DE NOEL

Traditionally this is filled with puréed chestnut and cream. Personally, I find it too rich, so I like cream and fruit. I sometimes use crystallised ginger and a little syrup from the jar. Frozen raspberries are wonderful at Christmas time.

FOR THE BASE:
6 eggs
5 oz/150g caster sugar
2 oz/50g cocoa powder, sieved
a little icing sugar

FOR THE FILLING:
4 oz/100g cream cheese
5 fl oz/150ml double cream
2 oz/50g caster sugar
glacé or fresh fruit pieces

FOR THE DECORATION:
1/2 pint/300ml double cream
2 oz/50g dark chocolate

Grease and base-line a Swiss roll tin 13"x9"/23x33cm. Separate the eggs. Put the whites in a large bowl. In another bowl, whisk the yolks until pale in colour and thick. Whisk in the sugar and cocoa. Clean and dry the whisk. Whisk the egg white until stiff but not dry. Fold in 1 tbsp egg white into the yolk mixture, then cut and fold the yolk mixture into the white until thoroughly combined. Spread the mixture evenly into the prepared tin.

For the two-oven Aga, put the shelf on the bottom set of runners in the roasting oven. Slide in the Swiss roll tin. Put the cold shelf onto the middle set of runners. For the four-oven Aga, put the oven shelf on the second set of runners from the bottom of the baking oven. Bake for 15-20 minutes until risen, puffy and springy in the centre. Remove from the oven and cool completely. Cut a piece of greaseproof paper slightly larger than the Swiss roll tin. Lay it on the work surface and sprinkle with caster or icing sugar. Loosen the chocolate base and turn out onto the paper. Remove the lining paper.

Put the cream cheese, sugar and cream into a bowl and beat well. Spread this mixture over the chocolate base. Sprinkle on diced fresh or glacé fruit. Roll up, using the greaseproof paper to help. Transfer to a plate. Stand a basin containing the chocolate on top of the Aga to warm. Whip the cream until just peaking. Spread evenly over the log. Drizzle over the melted chocolate up and down the length of the log. Fork over the chocolate to make it look like bark. Decorate with fresh holly.

Cuts 8-10 slices.

STOLLEN

....

Stollen is very popular at Christmas time, but the commercial varieties can be over-spiced. Try making your own. They can easily be frozen and decorated when thawed.

1 lb/450g strong white flour
2 oz/50g caster sugar
1/2 tsp salt
2 packets easy-blend yeast
6 fl oz/175ml warm milk
2 eggs, beaten
1 oz/25g melted butter
1 tsp almond essence
2 oz/50g chopped candied lemon peel
2 oz/50g chopped candied orange peel
grated rind 1 orange
grated rind 1 lemon
8 oz/225g marzipan
egg to glaze

Mix flour, sugar, salt and yeast together. Add milk, eggs, butter, essence, peel and rinds. Stir to make a smoothish dough. Transfer to a floured work surface and knead until the dough is smooth and elastic. Place dough in a bowl, cover with a cloth, stand on top of the Aga to rise. When doubled in size, knock back. Roll to an oblong approximately 12"x8"/20 x 30cm. Knead the marzipan and roll to a sausage 12"/30cm long. Place marzipan on the dough and roll the bread to form a 12"/30cm long loaf. Place seam side down on a greased baking sheet and cover. Place the loaf on top of the Aga to rise until doubled in size. Brush with egg glaze. Bake on the second set of runners from the top in the roasting oven for 25-30 minutes, until the loaf sounds hollow when tapped on the bottom. Remove from baking sheet and cool. If desired, pour on water icing, sprinkle with toasted, flaked almonds.

APRICOT AND ORANGE MINCEMEAT

The apricots and oranges give a good colour to this mincemeat. Use this to make the Macaroon Mince Pies.

8 oz/225g dried apricots
grated rind and juice of 1 orange
2 lb/1kg currants, sultanas and raisins, mixed
4 tbsp orange marmalade
1 lb/450g demerara sugar
8 oz/225g shredded suet
11/2 tsp ground mixed spice
3/4 tsp ground nutmeg
7 fl oz/250ml brandy

Soak apricots in cold water overnight. Drain them well, dry on kitchen paper and chop into smallish pieces. Mix the rind with apricots, dried fruit, marmalade, sugar, suet and spices. Stir in 3 tablespoons of orange juice and the brandy, and mix well. Cover and leave to stand for 24 hours. Press into jars and cover. Store in a cool place for up to 6 months.

GRANNY'S MINCEMEAT

This recipe for mincemeat has been handed down to me from my granny. It is a simple mincemeat and can be made in any quantities. If you make this two to three weeks before you need to use it, there is no need to heat to prevent fermentation, but if you are going to store it to allow the flavours to develop, a little heating stops the apple fermenting.

1 lb/450g soft brown sugar
1 lb/450g currants
1 lb/450g raisins
1 lb/450g suet, grated or shredded
1 lb/450g cooking apples, peeled, cored and grated
8 oz/225g candied peel, chopped
brandy or brandy and sherry mixed

In a large bowl, mix together the sugar, currants, raisins, suet, apple and candied peel. Mix them well. Place an oven-proof plate on top and put in the simmering oven for 3 hours. Remove, stir well and leave until completely cold, stirring occasionally. When cold, add enough brandy to make the mincemeat moist, about 10-15 tablespoons. Stir well and pack into clean, sterile jars. Seal and label.

Makes about 8 1lb/450g jars.

JEAN'S CHRISTMAS PUDDING

I was given this recipe by Jean Chapman, my first head of department when I started teaching Home Economics. Like the rest of us, she collects recipes, and she tells me this one is probably well over 100 years old. Do not be tempted to add eggs or liquids to this recipe.

21/2 lb/1.25kg raisins
1 lb/450g plain flour
1 lb/450g dark, soft brown sugar
1 lb/450g potatoes, peeled, boiled and mashed
1 lb/450g carrots, peeled and grated
1 lb/450g apples, peeled, cored and grated
1 lb/450g suet
grated rind and juice of 1 lemon and 1 orange
1/2 tsp bicarbonate of soda
1 tsp baking powder
1 tbsp brandy or rum
1 tsp ground allspice

Place all the ingredients in a large mixing bowl and mix very thoroughly together – I find this best done with my hand. Put the mixture in either 2 x 3-pint/2-litre pudding basins or 3 x 2-pint/1-litre pudding basins. Cover with a sheet of greaseproof paper and either a lid or a double thickness of foil. Stand the pudding on a trivet or old plate in a saucepan. Pour in 2"/5cm of water, put on the lid and bring to the boil on the boiling plate. When boiling, transfer to the simmering plate and allow to bubble gently for 30 minutes – you may need to pull the pan off the hot plate a little if it is bubbling away too rapidly. Transfer the saucepan to the simmering oven and leave to cook for 4-6 hours. Remove from the oven and allow to cool completely. When completely cold, replace the greaseproof paper with fresh paper and foil. Store in a cool place for up to 6 months. On the day of eating, simmer the pudding in a saucepan of water for 30 minutes, then transfer it to the simmering oven where it should steam for 2¹/₂ hours.

Serves 16.

LIGHT CHRISTMAS PUDDING

A good pudding to make at the last minute or make ahead and freeze, this is not rich enough to store out of the fridge.

3 oz/75g currants
3 oz/75g raisins
6 oz/175g sultanas
grated rind and juice of 1 orange
4 tbsp brandy
3 tbsp black treacle
6 oz/175g soft margarine
3 oz/75g dark soft brown sugar
3 eggs, beaten
6 oz/175g wholemeal flour
3 oz/75g fresh breadcrumbs
2 level tsp baking powder
3 oz/75g chopped hazelnuts
2 level tsp mixed spice

The day before making the cake, put the currants, raisins, sultanas, rind and juice of the orange, brandy and treacle together in a mixing bowl. Stir well, cover and leave to stand. In a mixing bowl, cream together the margarine and sugar until light and fluffy, beat in the eggs, a little at a time, with some of the flour. When all the eggs are mixed in, fold in the remaining ingredients and lastly the dried fruit mixture. Stir very well. Divide the mixture into two 2-pint/1-litre basins or one 3-pint/2-litre basin. Cover with a circle of greaseproof paper and either a plastic lid or foil.

Stand the pudding on a trivet or an old plate in the bottom of a deep saucepan. Pour in 2"/5cm of water, put on the lid and bring to the boil on the boiling plate. Transfer to the simmering plate and allow to bubble gently for 30 minutes – you may need to pull the pan off the plate a little if it is bubbling away too rapidly. Transfer to the simmering oven and leave for 3 hours for the smaller ones, 4 hours for the large one. Remove and allow to cool completely. When cold, replace the greaseproof with fresh paper and a new foil lid. Store in the fridge for up to one week, or freeze.

On the day of eating, bring to the boil and simmer for 30 minutes and then transfer to the simmering oven for $2^{1}/_{2}$ hours.

Serves 8-10.

GRANNY'S CHRISTMAS PUDDING

A very dark Christmas pudding of the old-fashioned type, this was always made at home the way Granny made it. Over the years, the fat has been reduced, but the end result will be dark and rich.

10 oz/275g shredded suet
12 oz/350g demerara sugar
1 lb/450g sultanas
1 lb/450g currants
1 lb/450g raisins
1 cooking apple, grated
1/2 oz/15g ground mixed spice
1/2 oz/15g ground ginger
pinch salt
grated rind and juice of 1 lemon
grated rind and juice of 1 orange
1/2 pint/300ml beer
1/2 pint/300ml water
2 fl oz/60ml brandy
1 fl oz/30ml sherry

1 fl oz/30ml rum
5 eggs, beaten
12 oz/350g fresh breadcrumbs

Mix everything together except the eggs and breadcrumbs. Cover and leave to stand for 3-4 days, stirring occasionally. When ready to cook, mix in the eggs and breadcrumbs and stir well. Spoon into 2 large (3-pint/2-litre) pudding basins or 3 medium (2-pint/1-litre) pudding basins. Cover with a sheet of greaseproof paper and either a lid or a double thickness of foil.

Stand the pudding on a trivet or old plate in a saucepan. Pour in 2"/5cm water, put on the lid and bring to the boil on the boiling plate. When boiling, transfer pan to the simmering plate and allow to bubble gently for 30 minutes – you may need to pull it off the hot plate a little if it is bubbling away too rapidly. Transfer to the simmering oven and leave to cook for 4-6 hours. Remove from the oven and allow to cool completely. When completely cold, replace the greaseproof paper and foil. Store in a cool place for up to 6 months.

On the day of eating, simmer for 30 minutes and then transfer to the simmering oven for $2\frac{1}{2}$ hours

Serves 16.

LITTLE CHRISTMAS PUDDINGS

....

These puddings can be made at the last minute or made a day or two in advance and re-heated when needed. Using home-made, sugar-free mincemeat avoids too much sweetness. Serve with pouring cream or brandy butter.

5 oz/150g self-raising flour
1 level tsp baking powder
1 round tsp ground mixed spice
2 oz/50g butter, softened
2 eggs
3 generous tbsp black treacle
2 tbsp brandy or rum
4 fl oz/100ml Guinness
1 lb/450g jar mincemeat
1 eating apple, peeled, cored and grated
grated zest of 1 orange and 1 lemon
6 oz/175g currants
1 oz/25g chopped, roasted nuts (almonds or hazelnuts)

Sieve the flour, baking powder and mixed spice into a mixing bowl. Add the butter, eggs, treacle, Guinness and brandy. Whisk the mixture well; this is best done with an electric whisk. Stir in the mincemeat, grated apple, lemon and orange rind, currants and nuts. Stir well. Butter the insides of 8 individual metal or foil pudding basins. Divide the pudding mixture between the buttered basins. Cut 8 squares of foil large enough to cover the tops of the basins. Butter them well. Place over the top of the basin, butter side down and tuck under well.

Stand the basins in the small roasting tin. Pour boiling water from the kettle around the little puddings until about ¹/₂"/1cm deep. Slide the roasting tin into the middle of the roasting oven and cook for 40-50 minutes. Cool in tins for 10 minutes before turning out onto a plate. To re-heat, stand the basins in the roasting tin, surround with boiling water and

....

return to the oven for 15-20 minutes. Do not leave the puddings in the metal basins for more than 24 hours.

Makes 8.

B R A N D Y   B U T T E R

This is so easy to make and can be kept for several weeks if made with fresh butter and stored in small, covered pots in the fridge. Serve with Christmas pudding and warm mince pies.

3 oz/75g unsalted butter
6 oz/175g sieved icing sugar or caster sugar
2 tbsp brandy

Cream together the butter and sugar until light and fluffy. Gradually beat in the brandy. Chill before serving.

Serves 8.

RUM BUTTER

....

This gives a darker, richer butter. It goes well with a lighter pudding.

4 oz/100g unsalted butter
4 oz/100g soft brown sugar
4 tbsp rum

Cream together the butter and sugar until pale in colour and fluffy in texture. Beat in the rum. Chill before serving.

Serves 6-8.

....

SHERRY SAUCE

....

For those who prefer a sauce rather than a butter to go with their Christmas pudding, this is a creamy mixture whish is easy to make and keep warm.

1 oz/25g butter
1 oz/25g flour
$^1/_2$ pint/300 ml single cream
1 oz/25g caster sugar
2-3 tbsp sherry

Melt the butter in a small pan, stir in the flour and cook for 1-2 minutes. Gradually stir in the cream and bring to the boil, stirring all the time. Remove from the heat and stir in the sherry. Add sugar according to taste – this will depend upon the type of sherry used. Taste and serve hot.

Serves 8.

....

CUSTARD SAUCE

This recipe is for a basic custard sauce, but to ring the changes add some orange rind and juice, or some brandy – or both! A well flavoured sauce is particularly good with a lighter, less rich Christmas pudding.

3 tbsp custard powder
2 tbsp sugar
1 pint/600ml milk
Additions:grated rind and juice of 2 oranges
2-3 tbsp brandy

In a small basin, blend together the custard powder and sugar to a paste with a little milk. In a saucepan, bring the remaining milk to the boil, pour onto the custard mixture. Stir well, return to the pan. Over a gentle heat bring to the boil whilst stirring. Allow to boil and thicken. Add the rind and juice of 2 oranges and the brandy, if using. Taste and adjust sugar if necessary.

Serves 8.

MUSHROOM FILO CUPS

These make a delicious vegetarian dish. Single cups can also be used as a starter. Try to use different types of mushrooms to add variety in appearance and flavour.

4 oz/100g butter
9 sheets filo pastry
8 oz/225g oyster mushrooms
8 oz/225g button brown cap mushrooms
salt and pepper
1/2 pint/300ml double cream
1 tbsp chopped parsley

Put 2 oz/50g butter in a basin and stand it on the Aga to melt. Use this to brush the sheets of filo. Cut the sheets of filo pastry in half. Use some of the melted butter to brush the insides of 6 ramekin or deep muffin dishes. Butter the sheets of filo and layer them 3 sheets at a time. Use them to line the ramekins, leaving the edges standing up for extra height. You should have enough filo pastry to line 6 ramekins. Bake on the floor of the roasting oven for 10-15 minutes until crisp and golden brown. Allow to cool in the ramekins. Slice the button mushrooms and fry gently in the remaining 2 oz/50g butter. When cooked transfer half the mushrooms to a liquidiser or processor. Add the oyster mushrooms to the mushrooms remaining in the pan and cook gently with a lid on for 5 minutes. Season with salt and pepper and add 4 tbsp single cream. Keep mixture warm.

For the sauce, process the button mushrooms in the liquidiser, pour into a small saucepan, add the remaining cream, chopped parsley, salt and pepper. Heat gently. Remove the filo cups from their moulds and place on a baking sheet, fill with the oyster mushroom mixture. Put the oven shelf on the floor of the roasting oven. Slide in the baking sheet and warm through for 5 minutes. Serve with some sauce round the cups.

Serves 6 as a starter or 3 as a main course.

QUAIL IN BACON

Quail are small birds with a mild, gamey flavour. Serve one as a starter or two as a main course. Everything is cooked in the oven and if cooking for a crowd prepare the bread rounds in advance, and reheat and crisp just before serving.

4 quail
salt and pepper
4 rashers streaky bacon with rinds trimmed off
4 slices white bread
1 oz/25g butter
1 tbsp cooking oil
watercress to garnish

Stretch the streaky bacon with the back of a table knife. Wrap one rasher of bacon round each quail. Place in the small roasting tin and hang on the second set of runners from the top of the roasting oven. Roast for 25-30 minutes until crisp, golden brown and cooked through.

Meanwhile prepare the bread. Cut each slice into a circle, use a pastry cutter if you have a large one. Put the butter and oil in a frying pan or on a thick, deep roasting tray and put on the floor of the roasting oven. When hot, fry the bread, turn over and fry the second side. When crisp and golden brown, put them on a warm serving plate, place a cooked quail on top, garnish with watercress and serve.

Serves 2 for a main course or 4 as a starter.

GLAZED GAMMON AND SPICED APRICOTS

Gammon cooked gently in the Aga will always be moist and tender. Served with spiced apricots, this joint can be served hot or cold. For a crowd increase the size of the joint, and the cooking time, and just make more spiced apricots. For the best flavour, prepare the apricots 24 hours in advance.

1 piece gammon about 3 lb/1¹/₂kg in weight
1 tbsp made mustard
2-3 tbsp demerara sugar
a few cloves

SPICED APRICOTS:
15 oz/425g can of apricot halves in fruit juice
3 tbsp white wine vinegar
3 oz/75g caster sugar
6-8 cloves
1"/2.5cm stick of cinnamon

Cook the gammon according to the instructions in the 'Basic Aga Techniques' section. Spread the mustard over the scored fat and press on the demerara sugar — this is easiest done by hand. Stud with the cloves. Place the ham in a roasting tin, glazed side uppermost. Hang the tin on the third set of runners from the top of the roasting oven and cook until the ham is glazed and golden brown — watch that it does not burn. Allow the ham to rest for 10-15 minutes before carving or allow to cool before slicing if serving cold. For the spiced apricots, drain the juice from the can into a measuring jug. Place the apricots in a bowl. Measure ¹/₄ pint/150ml juice into a small saucepan. Add the vinegar, sugar, cinnamon and cloves. Stir over a low heat until the sugar is dissolved. Bring to the boil and pour over the apricots. Allow to cool and stand for 24 hours before serving.

Serves 6.

ROAST GOOSE WITH APPLES

Goose is not always readily available, so give your butcher an order in advance. Serve with apples to give a fresh flavour.

9-11 lb/4-5kg oven-ready goose
salt and pepper
$^1/_2$ oz/15g butter
1 large onion, skinned and chopped
1 tbsp fresh sage, finely chopped
4 oz/100g fresh breadcrumbs
4 tbsp port
8 eating apples e.g. Cox
$^1/_2$ pint/300ml dry white wine

Prick the goose all over with a fork or a skewer. Remove any excess fat from the inside of the bird. Rub the skin with salt. If the goose has its giblets, remove and wash the liver and dice it. Melt the butter in a frying pan and cook the onion until softened, but not brown. Add the chopped liver and cook for a further 2-3 minutes. Stir in the port until bubbling then add the breadcrumbs, sage, salt and pepper. Mix well. Use the stuffing to stuff the goose's neck. Tie the bird and weigh it, and stand it on the rack in the roasting tin – the large one will probably be needed.

Roast on the second set of runners from the top of the roasting oven for 15 minutes per pound/450g plus 15 minutes, basting occasionally to allow a crisp skin to form. About 30 minutes before the end of cooking, drain the fat, core the apples and cut into quarters. Add to the roasting tin with the wine. Return to the oven. Serve the goose with the apples and juices.

Serves 8.

SAUSAGEMEAT STUFFING

Sausagemeat adds moisture to a turkey. Nowadays we should not stuff the body cavity of poultry, so I use some of this to stuff the neck end. It is firm when cooked and slices well. Any leftover mixture can be made into balls and cooked round the turkey towards the end of roasting. This is enough for a 10-12lb/4.5-5.4kg oven-ready turkey.

2lb/1kg sausagemeat
8 oz/225g streaky bacon, finely diced
1 large onion, peeled and finely chopped
¹/₂ oz/15g butter
1 level tbsp fresh sage, finely chopped

Melt the butter in a frying pan and cook the diced bacon and onion until soft but not browned. Put the sausagemeat in a mixing bowl, add the sage and cooked bacon and onion. Mix together well; I find this easiest to do with the hands. When well mixed, use to stuff the bird.

APPLE AND CELERY STUFFING

The fruit and celery make a good combination and can be used to stuff a turkey or go round a joint of roast pork.

1 oz/25g butter
2 onions, skinned and chopped
2 sticks celery, chopped
4 medium cooking apples, peeled, cored and finely chopped
3 oz/75g fresh white breadcrumbs
2 tbsp chopped parsley
salt and pepper

Melt the butter in a frying pan, add the celery and onion and cook until softening but not brown. Remove with a slotted spoon and put in a mixing bowl. Add the apple and cook until softening. Add to the onion and celery mixture, stir in the breadcrumbs, parsley, salt and pepper. Press together if making stuffing balls, or stuff the neck end of a turkey.

CHRISTMAS

SHERRIED TURKEY GRAVY

....

This rich gravy adds lots of flavour to the turkey. It is especially useful as it can be made the day before and refrigerated until needed.

2 tbsp olive oil
all the turkey giblets, chopped to fit in a pan
1 oz/25g flour
2 tsp tomato purée
1¹/₂ pints/1 litre chicken stock or 2 cubes made up to that amount
5 fl oz/150ml amontillado sherry
salt and pepper
bouquet garni of fresh herbs

Heat the oil in a roomy saucepan, stir in the giblets and brown well. Add the tomato purée and flour, and use this to coat the giblets. Continue stirring and add the stock, sherry, a seasoning of salt and pepper and the bouquet garni. Put a lid on the pan, bring to the boil and, once boiling, transfer to the simmering oven for 1 hour. Remove from the oven and strain. Chill and store in the fridge, or use immediately. Remove the turkey from the roasting tin and put on a plate, keeping warm. Skim any excess fat from the tin, then pour in the giblet gravy. Stand the tin on the simmering plate and bring to the boil, stirring. Bubble until the required thickness. Serve hot.

Serves 8.

....

C R A N B E R R Y   S A U C E

The colour of cranberry sauce is attractive on the Christmas table. It is even delicious served with cold meats. This sauce will not keep for long, so if you want to make the most of cranberries in the shops you will need to freeze any extra fruit. This is quick and easy to make, and much nicer than anything from a jar.

4 oz/100g caster sugar
5 fl oz/150ml water
finely grated rind of 1 orange
8 oz/225g fresh cranberries

Wash and pick over the cranberries, removing any stalks, grit and shrivelled fruits. In a saucepan, place the sugar and water. Stand the pan over a gentle heat and stir to dissolve the sugar. Add the orange rind and cranberries. Cover with a lid and cook over a low heat until the cranberries are cooked – you can usually hear them bursting. This takes 8-10 minutes. Stir well and serve warm, or refrigerate until needed.

Serves 8.

BREAD SAUCE

....

This is one of the traditional accompaniments for roast turkey. It will withstand being made the day before and warming through. Add the cream just before serving.

4 oz/100g fresh breadcrumbs
1 onion
6 cloves
1 bayleaf
6 whole black peppercorns
1 pint/600ml milk
2 oz/50ml butter
1-2 tbsp single cream
salt and pepper

Stick the onion with the cloves. Put into a medium saucepan with the milk, bayleaf and peppercorns. Slowly bring the milk to the boil. Remove from the heat and leave to stand at the back of the Aga for at least 30 minutes. Strain the milk into a clean saucepan. Warm through and stir in the breadcrumbs and butter. Beat well until the butter has melted. Check the seasoning. Stir in the cream and serve.

Serves 8.
....

CRANBERRY CHUTNEY

Cranberries are available at Christmas and this recipe makes a chutney that looks festive on the plate with cold meats and cheeses. Make about one month before it's needed. It makes an attractive present.

1 1/2 lb/700g fresh cranberries
1/2 pint/300ml malt vinegar
8 oz/225g sultanas
4 oz/100g raisins
4 oz/100g sugar
1/2 oz/15g salt
2 tsp allspice
2 tsp ground cinnamon

Wash and pick over the cranberries. Place them in a saucepan with the remaining ingredients and stir over a gentle heat until the sugar has dissolved. Bring to simmering point. Cover and transfer to the simmering oven for 45 minutes to 1 hour, until the mixture has thickened. Pour into warm, sterile jars. Seal when cold with acid-resistant tops. Keeps for 6 months.

KATE'S TRIFLE

A delicious variation on the traditional English trifle theme, this was made by Kate for a smart picnic at the height of the summer in Stourhead Gardens. I have made it at Christmas and for dinner parties.

FOR THE SPONGE:

3 oz/75g caster sugar
3 eggs
3 oz/75g self-raising flour
a little extra caster sugar

FOR THE TRIFLE:

15 oz/425g can unsweetened apricots
5 fl oz/150ml Marsala or pale cream sherry and brandy mixed
4 oz/100g plain chocolate, melted
2 tbsp cornflour
2 tbsp caster sugar
2 eggs, beaten
$^1/_2$ pint/300ml milk
3 oz/75g macaroons, crumbled
1 pint/600ml double cream
chocolate buttons – to decorate
split almonds – to decorate

To make the sponge, grease and line a 12" x 9"/30 x 22cm Swiss roll tin. Sieve the flour onto a plate. Place the eggs and sugar in a bowl and whisk, using an electric whisk, until thick and foamy, thick enough to leave a trail. Sieve the flour and fold it into the mixture with a table-spoon, using a cut-and-fold motion. Take care not to knock out the air, so that you keep a light, fluffy mixture. Pour the mixture into the Swiss roll tin. Allow to level off in the tin. Place the oven shelf on the floor of the roasting oven. Put in the Swiss roll and bake for 8 minutes until evenly brown and springy to the touch.

Lay a sheet of greaseproof paper – slightly larger than the cake tin – on the work surface and sprinkle with caster sugar. When baked, remove the cake from the oven and immediately tip out onto the sugared greaseproof paper. Peel off the lining carefully.

Drain the apricots. Purée the fruit. Cut the sponge cake in half and use $1/2$ the apricot purée to sandwich the cake halves together. Cut the layered cake into strips 1" x 2"/2.5 x 5cm. Arrange the cake in the bottom of a glass serving dish. Pour the Marsala or sherry mixture over the sponge cake in the dish. Spread on the remaining apricot purée. Drizzle the melted chocolate over it and spread evenly over the apricot purée.

Prepare the custard. In a saucepan, measure in the cornflour and sugar, and blend in the milk. Stand the pan on the simmering plate and heat, whisking all the time until the custard thickens. Remove from the heat and whisk in the beaten eggs. Return to the heat, whisking, and heat through, but do not allow to boil. Remove from the heat and whisk in the crumbled macaroons. Allow to cool, whisking periodically to blend in the macaroons. Pour the custard over the sponge mixture. Chill.

About one hour before serving, whisk the cream to the soft peak stage. Carefully spread this on top of the custard mixture. Decorate with chocolate buttons and split almonds.

MACAROON MINCE PIES

The macaroon topping ensures that the pies do not have too much pastry. These are lighter than most mince pies, and taste particularly delicious when made with apricot and orange mincemeat. The same quantity will fill a 4¹/₂" x 14"/35 x 11cm tranche tin.

8 oz/225g sweet shortcrust pastry
8 oz/225g mincemeat
2 egg whites
3 oz/75g caster sugar
4 oz/100g ground almonds
greased 12 bun tin

Roll out the chilled pastry and stamp out about 12 rounds with a 3"/7.5cm cutter and line bun tins. Fill the pastry cases with mincemeat. Whisk the egg whites until stiff but not dry. Whisk in the sugar a little at a time. Fold in the ground almonds. Divide the mixture between the tins, covering the mincemeat well. Bake on the floor of the roasting oven for about 15 minutes until golden brown. Cool on a wire rack. Dust with a little icing sugar. Serve warm or cold.

Makes about 12.

STILTON SOUP

Bits of Stilton are often left over after Christmas. I find this a useful way of using up leftovers. Use turkey stock if you have made some. This recipe makes a thick, very creamy soup, but if you want a thinner soup just add more stock.

1 onion, peeled and chopped
4 sticks celery, trimmed and chopped
1 oz/25g butter
1 oz/25g flour
1 pint/600ml light stock
8 oz/225g blue Stilton, chopped

Melt the butter in a saucepan, add the onion and celery and cook until softening. Stir in the flour, cook for 1 minute, stirring continuously. Slowly add the stock, still stirring, and bring to the boil. Add the chopped Stilton, stir and return to the boil. Cover and transfer to the simmering oven for 20-30 minutes. Remove from the oven and liquidise or process the soup until smooth. Check seasoning and serve.

Serves 4.

HAM AND CHEESE MILLEFEUILLE

Any leftover ham or turkey can be used for this recipe. The minced ham can be replaced with the same quantity of other cold, cooked, minced meat.

1 lb/450g puff pastry
8 oz/225g onion, finely chopped
6 oz/175g eating apple, grated
6 oz/175g ham, minced coarsely
2 oz/50g butter
1 bay leaf
2 oz/50g frozen chopped spinach
1 oz/25g flour
$1/_2$ pint/300ml milk
6 oz/175g Gruyère cheese, grated
1 grating of nutmeg
pepper
beaten egg for glazing

Roll out half the pastry to an oblong about 11" x 5"/28 x 12.5cm. Place on a baking sheet and prick it all over with a fork. Bake in the roasting oven on the second set of runners from the top for 15-20 minutes until risen and golden brown.

Prepare a sauce with half the butter melted in a saucepan. Stir in the flour and spinach. Cook for 1-2 minutes, then stir in the milk, nutmeg and pepper. Boil until thickened and stir in half the grated cheese. Set aside to cool. Melt the remaining butter in a saucepan and sauté the onion. When softening, add the grated apple and bay leaf, cover and cook gently in the simmering oven for 15 minutes.

To assemble, spoon the onion mixture over the pastry base. Top with the ham followed by the spinach sauce. Sprinkle over the remaining cheese. Roll the remaining pastry to an oblong slightly larger than the base.

Carefully lay this on top of the filling and tuck under any raw pastry edges to make a secure parcel. Brush the pastry well with the egg glaze, mark a lattice pattern over the pastry. Sprinkle with coarse sea salt.

Bake with the shelf on the bottom set of runners of the roasting oven. Slide in the baking tray and bake for 30-40 minutes until pastry is puffed and golden brown. Serve warm.

Serves 6-8.

TURKEY AND LEEK CRUMBLE

A moist way to use up any leftovers of turkey. Pieces of ham could also be added. Strip the meat from the turkey and cut into bite-sized pieces.

1 oz/25g butter
1 oz/25g flour
15 fl oz/450ml milk
salt and pepper
1 tsp fresh sage, finely chopped
1 lb/450g leeks, trimmed, washed and sliced
4 oz/100g mushrooms wiped and sliced
1 lb/450g cold, cooked turkey

CRUMBLE:
2 oz/50g butter
4 oz/100g wholemeal flour
1 tsp mustard powder
2 oz/50g tasty cheese – grated
1 oz/25g porridge oats

Melt 1oz/25g butter in a saucepan and stir in the leeks. Cook gently until softening. Add the mushrooms and cook for a further 1-2 minutes. Drain and place in an oven-proof dish. Add the turkey to the vegetables. Stir the 1 oz/25g flour into the remaining butter in the pan, whisk in the milk to make a sauce. When thickened, add the sage and season with salt and pepper. Pour over the meat mixture.

For the crumble, rub the butter into the flour and stir in remaining ingredients. Sprinkle the crumble over the meat mixture. Bake with the shelf on the bottom set of runners in the roasting oven for 25-30 minutes until golden brown and bubbling hot.

Serves 4

HOGMANAY OR NEW YEAR'S EVE

In Scotland and the North of England, Hogmanay is the time for celebration and party-giving. Seeing in the New Year is becoming more popular in the rest of England, too, and is perhaps a time to invite friends for a party after the family time at Christmas.

I have chosen typically Scottish fare, as Scotland produces some beautiful food and drink not always encountered south of the border. The beef dish and the venison require last-minute cooking, so if you're catering for a crowd, a venison casserole may be easier to manage. I give the instructions for cooking haggis and its traditional accompaniments. I know that this is the traditional dish for Burns' night, but some people do like haggis at New Year.

Start the evening with Scottish fish like fresh or smoked salmon or Finnan haddock, a lovely smoked fish pale yellow in colour. A creamy pudding with oatmeal and Scottish raspberries will make a lovely light dessert, before ending the meal with a selection of Scottish cheeses such as Dunlop, Crowdie or Howgate to go with home-made oatcakes.

After first-footing, have a small slice of Black Bun – made weeks in advance to mature – with a dram of whisky.

TWO SALMON TERRINE

Make this either in six individual ramekin dishes or in a small loaf tin. Chill and slice to serve either as a starter or fish course. No raw eggs are used so this is safe for the elderly, pregnant women and children.

8 oz/225g smoked salmon
8 oz/225g cooked salmon
1 tbsp brandy
4 oz/100g butter, softened
juice 1 lemon
salt and pepper

Use half the smoked salmon to line the ramekin dishes or loaf tin – they do not need to be completely lined. Pound together the remaining ingredients, if using a food processor be careful not to lose the textures by over-processing. Taste and adjust the seasoning. Divide the mixture between the ramekins or put in the loaf tin. Press down and smooth the top. Cover and chill for 2-3 hours or even overnight. Turn out onto plates, or cut slices from the 'loaf' and garnish with salad leaves. Serve with freshly baked bread or hot toast.

Serves 6.

VENISON AND WALNUT CASSEROLE

Venison makes a rich casserole, perfect for winter entertaining. All venison can be used, but some find it too rich. The walnuts and prunes add a variety of textures. Like many casseroles, this has a more mature flavour if made the day before and re-heated. Serve with creamy potatoes and peas.

1 lb/450g braising steak
1 lb/450g braising venison
10 oz/275g no-soak prunes
5 fl oz/150ml port
1 large onion, chopped
2 level tbsp flour
1 level tsp ground cinnamon
1/2 pint/300ml beef stock
salt and pepper
2 tbsp balsamic vinegar
4 oz/100g walnut halves
1 tbsp cooking oil

Cut the meat into bite-sized portions. Place in a mixing bowl. Add the prunes and the port. Cover and leave the marinade for at least an hour or overnight. Heat the cooking oil in a flameproof casserole on the simmering plate and cook the onion until softened. Remove the onion and set aside. Transfer the casserole to the boiling plate, drain the meat from the marinade and brown the meat to seal. When all the meat is browned, return the onions, move casserole to the simmering plate and stir in the flour, cinnamon and salt and pepper. Cook for 1 minute then stir in the stock and the strained marinade, and finally the vinegar. Bring the casserole to the boil, cover and transfer to the simmering oven. Cook for 2 hours then stir in the reserved prunes and walnuts. Return to the oven for a further hour. Taste and adjust the seasoning.

Serves 8.

BEEF IN WHISKY SAUCE

Whisky and prime beef are two of Scotland's best products. In this recipe they combine well to make a wonderful special-occasion main course. Because the meat is cooked quickly, use a good sirloin steak for flavour and tenderness.

The recipe serves 4, but it can easily be multiplied to serve 12 or 16. Have the largest frying pan possible available. Batches of meat can be kept warm in the simmering oven after cooking, then returned to the pan when the liqueur and cream are added.

1 oz/25g butter
1½ lb/750g sirloin steak, cut into thin strips
1 large onion, skinned and chopped
3 tbsp Drambuie or whisky
3 fl oz/75ml double cream
salt and pepper

Melt the butter in the frying pan and cook the onion and beef for 5-10 minutes until the meat is brown and cooked to taste. Stir in the whisky and cream, heat through and bubble gently until a sauce is formed. Season to taste. Serve immediately with brown rice and green vegetables.

HAGGIS

....

Haggis is usually eaten on Burns' Night, however some people do like it for Hogmanay. Haggis is usually bought ready prepared because getting all the 'bits' can be difficult unless you are lucky enough to have a really good butcher.

1 haggis

Use a steamer if you have one, or put the haggis in a pudding basin and cover with a lid of foil. Stand the basin in a saucepan with a trivet. Pour in about 2"/5cm water and cover. Bring the pan to the boil, transfer to the simmering plate and simmer for 20 minutes. Transfer to the simmering oven for 2 hours until cooked and piping hot. Serve with clapshot.

CLAPSHOT

....

This root vegetable dish is usually served with haggis. In Scotland, the orange-fleshed root vegetable is known as turnip, further south it is called swede. The two colours, orange and white look attractive together.

1¹/₂ lb/750g potatoes, peeled and roughly chopped
1¹/₂ lb/750g swedes, peeled and roughly chopped
salt and pepper
1 oz/25g butter

Place the vegetables in a large saucepan. Add water to come half-way up the vegetables. Add some salt. Cover and bring to the boil. Drain and put into the simmering oven, cook until the vegetables are soft enough to mash. Remove from the oven and drain well. Mash with butter. Serve hot.

Serves 6.
....

OATMEAL AND YOGHURT CREAMS

An easy-to-make dessert keeping the Scottish theme. I think these creams improve if made an hour or two in advance, but they are equally good for a last-minute extra pudding.

3 oz/75g almonds, finely chopped
3 oz/75g medium oatmeal
2 oz/50g dark, soft brown sugar
1 lemon, rind grated and the juice squeezed
1 large carton natural yoghurt – Greek style is best
1/2 pint/300ml double cream, lightly whipped
2 tbsp flaked almonds, lightly toasted

Mix together the chopped almonds and oatmeal and spread the mixture out on a baking tray. Put the oven shelf on the highest setting in the roasting oven and put in the tray of almond mixture. Toast until golden. WATCH as it is easy to burn. Shake around the mixture to toast it evenly; this takes about 3-5 minutes. Leave to cool. Mix together the sugar, lemon rind and juice. Fold into the yoghurt. Gently fold in the almond mixture and finally the whipped cream. Spoon into 8 individual glasses or dishes and chill. Decorate with the toasted flaked almonds and a Scottish raspberry or two if you can find them!

Serves 8.

WHIM WHAM

....

This is a simple last-minute trifle made in the 18th century in Scotland. It means something light and fanciful. The addition of plain yoghurt makes it less rich.

1 oz/25g butter
2 oz/50g blanched almonds
1 oz/25g sugar
30 sponge fingers
5 fl oz/150ml sweet sherry
4 tbsp brandy
grated rind and juice of 1 orange
$1/_2$ pint/300ml double cream
10 oz/275g plain yoghurt

In a heavy frying pan, melt the butter and fry the almonds until golden brown. Stir in the sugar and cook, stirring, until the almonds are well coated with the melting sugar. Tip onto a greased baking sheet and cool.
About 30 minutes before serving, break the sponge fingers into a serving bowl. Mix the sherry, brandy, orange rind and juice and pour over the sponge fingers. Leave to stand. Whip the cream until it just holds its shape. Fold in the yoghurt and spoon the mixture on top of the sponge fingers. Roughly break up the almonds and scatter over the top.

Serve 6.
....

CARAMEL ORANGES

....

Oranges and tangerines are plentiful around Christmas time. Use either sliced oranges or whole, peeled tangerines, satsumas etc. The fruit tastes best if left to marinade in the caramel syrup for 24 hours. The caramel can be made a week in advance and stored for later use, and is therefore easy to increase for serving at a party. Serve with cream or yoghurt or even home-made ice-cream.

6 oz/175g granulated sugar
15 fl oz/450ml water
6 large oranges or 12 tangerines, peeled of all white pith

Put the sugar in a heavy based pan. Stand it on the simmering plate and cook slowly until the sugar has caramelised – do not stir. When it is golden, remove from the heat and pour in the water – be careful, the caramel may spit. Return to the heat and stir to make a caramel syrup. When the caramel is dissolved remove from the heat. Slice the oranges or separate the tangerine segments and lay them out in a serving dish. Pour on the caramel and cover. Allow to stand for at least 8 hours.

Serves 6.

....

OATCAKES

Oats are grown in Scotland and therefore used a lot in Scottish cookery. These oatcakes are simple to make and delicious with a range of Scottish cheeses.

4 oz/100g fine oatmeal
pinch salt
pinch bicarbonate of soda
$1/_2$ oz/15g lard
5 fl oz/150 ml water
oatmeal for rolling

Put the oatmeal, salt and bicarbonate of soda in a mixing bowl. Heat the lard and $1/_4$ pint/150ml water in a small saucepan until the lard has melted. Pour immediately onto the oatmeal mixture, to make a firm dough. Roll out the dough on a work surface sprinkled lightly with oatmeal to about $1/_8$"/3 mm thick. Stamp out 3"/7.5cm rounds or roll one large circle and cut triangles. Lightly oil the clean simmering plate. Place on the oatcakes, about 6 at a time for 5-8 minutes until cooked through – do not turn them over. If you know your simmering plate is hot, lift the lid for a couple of minutes before cooking. The oatcakes will curl up and become firm and dry when cooked. Cool on a wire rack.

Makes 1 dozen.

BLACK BUN

....

Black Bun is traditionally eaten at Hogmanay in Scotland. It is a rich fruit mixture enclosed in a pastry case. For ease of cutting, use a square cake tin, but a round one is just as good. Make this at least a month before eating, to allow the flavours to mature.

12 oz/350g plain flour
1/2 level tsp baking powder
pinch salt
4 oz/100g butter
cold water to bind the dough
egg to glaze

FILLING:
8 oz/225g plain flour
1/4 tsp black pepper
1 tsp ground cinnamon
1/2 tsp cream of tartar
1/4 tsp bicarbonate of soda
4 oz/100g caster sugar
1 lb/450g raisins
1 lb/450g currants
4 oz/100g blanched, chopped almonds
5 fl oz/150ml milk
1 tbsp brandy

Sieve the flour, baking powder and salt into a mixing bowl. Rub in the butter to resemble breadcrumbs. Bind the mixture together with cold water to make a firm dough. Divide the dough into 3 equal portions. Roll out two squares to fit a 7"/22cm square cake tin. Roll the remaining dough to fit round the sides of the tin and as deep as the tin – it is easier to do this in two strips. Grease the tin and line the base with one pastry square. Use the strips to line the sides, and make sure a good seal is made between the base and the sides.

To make the filling, sieve the flour, spices, cream of tartar, bicarbonate of soda and sugar together in a large bowl. Add the raisins, currants and nuts. Mix well. Stir in the milk and brandy and stir the mixture very well. Press this mixture into the pastry-lined tin. Top with the remaining pastry square, press down gently and seal the edges well. Prick all over with a fork and brush with the beaten egg.

Place the oven shelf on the floor of the roasting oven, put in the black bun and bake for half an hour. For the two-oven Aga, transfer to the simmering oven for 6-8 hours. For the four-oven Aga, bake with the shelf on the bottom set of runners in the baking oven for 2-2$\frac{1}{2}$ hours – cover with foil if becoming too brown. Cool in the tin and store either in a cake tin or wrapped in foil for at least 1 month before eating.

LENT AND EASTERTIDE

Lent is a time of fasting, and then there is a burst of joy and feasting at Easter. Traditionally eggs and milk were not eaten during Lent, so the day before Ash Wednesday these had to be used up, hence Pancake Day or Shrove Tuesday. Pancakes can, of course, be eaten all year round, and not just with sugar and lemon. You will find a range of recipes in this chapter to suit all tastes.

Hot Cross Buns are usually eaten on Good Friday, hence the cross. These are just a spiced bun with some sort of cross on. The commercial variety are available in the shops almost as soon as Christmas is over, but try making your own – they are very simple and they taste much nicer!

Fish is usually eaten on Good Friday. A simple smoked haddock dish is good with potatoes and vegetables.

Easter Sunday is a good time to invite friends to lunch and indulge in tender, pink spring lamb. Unless Easter is very early, fresh spring vegetables will also be available to give you a taste of things to come.

Simnel cakes, though now usually eaten as Easter cakes, were made by daughters in service and taken home for the annual visit on Mid Lent Sunday. Whenever you eat your Simnel cake it is a real marzipan-lover's delight.

PANCAKES

Today we eat pancakes at all times of the year, and they can be eaten both with a savoury filling or the more traditional lemon juice and sugar. Try to use a heavy-based pan for pancakes, and remember that the first pancake often does not work too well. A stack of pancakes can be made in advance and frozen, especially useful if they are for filling at a later date.

4 oz/100g plain flour
pinch salt
1 egg
about ¹/₂ pint/300ml milk
oil for frying

Either place the flour, salt, egg and milk in a food processor and whizz to a batter or place the flour and salt in a mixing bowl. Gradually beat in the egg and the milk slowly to make a smooth batter. The batter should be the consistency of thick cream.

Heat a large, solid-based pan on the boiling plate. Pour in a little oil and wipe it round with a wad of kitchen paper. Spoon in 2-3 tablespoons batter and swirl around the pan. Cook for about a minute; lift the edge with a palette knife, if browning underneath toss the pancake over and cook the second side for about 1 minute. Serve on a warm plate or keep hot in the simmering oven. Re-grease the pan after 2 or 3 pancakes.

Makes about 8.

SOUFFLÉ PANCAKES

You will need a good strong pan to make these, but they make a delicious dessert. Do not be too ambitious and make them only when cooking for a small number of guests.

5 oz/150g plain flour
2 oz/50g caster sugar
3 eggs, separated
1/2 tsp vanilla essence
15 fl oz/450ml milk
butter for cooking
jam or fruit compote
icing sugar

Stand the jam or compote in a basin on top of the Aga to warm and soften. Sieve the flour into a mixing bowl, stir in the sugar and make a well in the centre of the flour mixture. Add the egg yolks and some of the milk. Whisk or beat in, gradually adding more milk to make a smooth batter. Beat in the vanilla essence. Whisk the egg white until white and fluffy but not stiff. Beat 1 tablespoon egg white into the batter and then gently fold in the remaining egg white.

Heat the pan on the boiling plate. Transfer to the simmering plate and add enough butter to grease the pan. Pour in enough batter to cover the base of the pan and cook the pancake until set, flip over and cook the second side briefly. Slip onto a warm plate or dish, spread softened, warm jam or fruit compote over half the pancake and fold over the second half. Keep warm in the simmering oven. Repeat using all the batter. Dust with icing sugar and serve.

Makes 6 large pancakes.

CRÊPES

French-style crêpes make a change from traditional English pancakes. These should be so thin that you can almost see through them. You will need a good, heavy pan for even cooking, and the batter must be made at least 30 minutes before cooking. Use water, orange juice or beer as the liquid, depending upon what you fill your crêpes with.

4 oz/100g plain flour
2 eggs, beaten
1 tbsp oil
pinch salt
$^1/_2$ pint/300ml water, orange juice or beer
vegetable oil for frying

Place all the ingredients together in a blender or processor and whizz until smooth. Alternatively put the flour in a mixing bowl, gradually beat in the eggs and oil, followed by the liquid. Leave to stand for 30 minutes.

Heat a large, solid frying pan on the boiling plate. Pour in a little oil and wipe around with a wad of kitchen paper. Pour in a little batter, about 1-2 tablespoons depending upon the size of the pan, and swirl and tilt around to cover the base with batter. When the pancake curls around the edges toss over to cook on the other side for about 30 seconds. Serve on a warm plate. Every 2-3 pancakes re-oil the pan.

Makes about 10.

FLUFFY DROP SCONES

....

These are particularly nice with crispy bacon and maple syrup! But of course, they are good with butter and jam as well. They are light but substantial, and make a change from Scotch pancakes, though they're cooked in the same way.

8 oz/225g self-raising flour
$^1/_2$ tsp bicarbonate of soda
pinch salt
3 eggs, separated
12 fl oz/375ml milk
2 oz/50g caster sugar – optional
oil for greasing

Sieve the flour, salt and bicarbonate of soda together into a bowl. Add the egg yolks and gradually beat in the milk to make a batter. Whisk the egg whites until fluffy but not dry. Beat 1 tablespoon egg white into the batter, then fold the remaining egg white into the batter carefully. Lift the lid of the simmering plate, brush clean and then wipe over with some cooking oil on a wad of kitchen paper. Space tablespoonfuls of mixture over the simmering plate, about 5 at a time. The scones will rise and puff up. Turn over and cook the second side. When golden brown, place on warm serving plate or in a napkin to keep warm. Serve piled up with golden syrup or maple syrup.

Makes about 15-20, depending upon the size.
....

HOT CROSS BUNS

Hot cross buns are traditionally eaten on Good Friday. These are easy to make and taste much nicer than the commercial variety. You can make a cross with strips of shortcrust pastry but I tend to just cut a cross as I find the pastry often falls off!

1 lb/450g strong flour
1 tsp salt
1 tsp ground mixed spice
$1/_2$ tsp grated nutmeg
2 oz/50g caster sugar
$1/_2$ oz/15g fresh yeast
$1/_2$ pint/300ml warm milk
3 oz/75g butter
4 oz/100g currants
1 egg, beaten
Glaze: 3 tbsp caster sugar
3 tbsp milk

Blend the yeast with 1 teaspoon caster sugar and a little warm milk. Stand on warm (not hot) spot on the Aga and allow to froth while preparing the remaining ingredients. Into a large mixing bowl measure the flour, salt, mixed spice, nutmeg and sugar. Rub in the butter, stir in the currants. In a well in the middle of the flour and dry ingredients add the egg and yeast mixture and most of the milk. Beat together to make a soft dough, adding milk as needed. Turn onto a lightly floured work surface. Knead for about 5 minutes until the dough is smooth and elastic and put into a clean bowl. Stand the bowl on a tea towel folded on top of the simmering plate lid and cover with a clean tea towel. Leave until doubled in size.

Return the dough to a floured work top, gently knock back and divide the dough into 12 equal portions. Shape each into a roll and place on a greased and floured baking tray. Stand again on the simmering plate lid until doubled in size. Use a sharp knife to cut a cross in each roll. Bake on the third set of runners from the top of the roasting oven for about 15-20

minutes until golden and sounding hollow when tapped on the bottom.

Make the glaze: put the sugar and milk in a small saucepan and bring to the boil. Brush over the buns to form a sticky glaze. Cool the buns on a wire rack.

Makes 12 buns.

SMOKED HADDOCK AU GRATIN

I find this popular Good Friday fish dish often eaten throughout the year. This is easy to make in large quantities in the roasting tin if cooking for a crowd. Serve with new or mashed potatoes and a green vegetable.

2 lb/1kg smoked haddock fillet
1/2 pint/300ml milk
1 oz/25g butter
4 large tomatoes, sliced
5 fl oz/150ml single cream
4 oz/100g mature Cheddar or Gruyère, grated
black pepper

Place the fish in the small roasting tin. Pour on the milk. Slide the tin onto the bottom set of runners of the roasting oven and cook for 15-20 minutes until just flaking. Drain the fish, skin and break into large chunks. Place in an oven-proof dish. Season with pepper. Pour over the cream, lay on the tomatoes and sprinkle with the grated cheese. Return to the oven with the shelf on the bottom set of runners and bake for 20 minutes until golden brown.

Serves 6.

CHICKEN WITH WATERCRESS SAUCE

I serve this chicken dish at Easter when home-grown watercress has a fresh, distinctive flavour. The green sauce looks attractive with a selection of new vegetables.

6 chicken breasts – with bone
2 spring onions
2 oz/50g butter
1 tbsp oil
$^1/_2$ pint/300ml chicken stock
5 fl oz/150ml double cream
2 tbsp chopped watercress
salt and pepper

Heat the oil and butter in a large frying pan. Brown the chicken breasts, 2 or 3 at a time and place them in casserole. Add the onion to the pan and cook until golden. Add the stock, bring to the boil and pour onto the chicken. If your casserole dish is flameproof, put it on the simmering plate and bring everything to the boil. Transfer to the simmering oven. If your dish is not flameproof, put the casserole in the roasting oven for 15 minutes until the mixture is piping hot. Transfer to the simmering oven. Cook for 45 minutes – 1 hour until the chicken is cooked. Remove the chicken to a warm serving dish. Keep warm. Add the cream to the cooking liquor. Bring to the boil and bubble until reduced by half. Stir in the watercress and season to taste. Spoon over the chicken. Serve with steamed baby vegetables.

Serves 6.

ROAST LAMB

Roast lamb is perfect for Easter time. Good English or Welsh lamb should be available at the butchers and goes well with new potatoes and fresh young vegetables. A larger joint is best to roast and with the bone the meat will be sweeter. Joints of meat have little fat these days, so a smearing of lard is necessary to start the roasting process. I give the times here for a joint of 3 lb/1.5kg, but look up the chart at the beginning of the book for timing of other sized joints.

3 lb/1¹/₂kg leg of lamb
1¹/₂ oz/35g lard
4-6 sprigs rosemary

Smear the leg of lamb with the lard, and put it in the small roasting tin on top of the sprigs of rosemary. Put in the roasting oven on the third set of runners from the top. Cook for 1-1¹/₂ hours, depending upon the pinkness that you like. Half-way through roasting, remove from the oven and baste the joint with the fat surrounding it. Return to the oven and continue cooking. Remove from the oven when cooked – allow it to rest while making the gravy.

To make the gravy, remove the joint from the roasting tin and put it on a warm plate in the simmering oven to rest before carving. Skim off any excess fat from the roasting tin, leaving behind the juices. Stir in one tablespoon flour and cook it on the simmering plate, stirring well. Add about 1 pint of stock or vegetable cooking water and stir while boiling to the preferred consistency. Season. Pour into a hot gravy jug and skim off any excess fat.

MINT SAUCE

....

a good bunch of mint
2 tsp caster sugar
1 tbsp boiling water
3 tbsp wine vinegar

Snip the leaves off the stems of mint. Chop the leaves finely. Place in a small jug or basin. Add the sugar and then the boiling water – this retains the colour of the mint as well as dissolving the sugar. Add the vinegar and stir well. Do not prepare too long in advance, because the mint tends to turn brown.

NEW POTATOES

....

new potatoes
mint
butter
salt

Wash the potatoes but leave the skins on. Place the potatoes in a saucepan, pour in water to come 1-2"/3-5cm up the side of the pan. Add a good pinch of salt and two or three sprigs of mint. Cover and stand on the boiling plate and bring to the boil. Boil for 1 minute, drain off the water, re-cover and place in the simmering oven. New potatoes are difficult to judge, about 30-40 minutes depending upon the variety and size. If they are ready before you are, toss in butter and keep warm in the simmering oven. Serve with butter and chopped mint.

NEW VEGETABLES

If these are very small, simply plunge them into boiling, salted water and cook quickly, alternatively steam in a steamer over a pan of boiling water. Toss in butter and serve. Large root vegetables can be cooked like the potatoes.

CHOCOLATE TART

A rich chocolate dessert. Serve small slices only!

8 oz/225g sweet shortcrust pastry
8 oz/225g dark plain chocolate, chopped
$1/_2$ pint/300ml double cream
1 egg and 1 egg yolk
5 fl oz/150ml milk
cocoa powder and icing sugar to decorate

Roll out the pastry and use to line a deep 8"/20cm flan tin, preferably loose-bottomed. Chill for half an hour. Brush the pastry case with the egg yolk. Mix the remaining yolk with the whole egg and the milk. Boil the cream, remove from the heat and beat in the chocolate until melted. Beat into the egg mixture and pour into the prepared flan case. It is easier to stand the flan case on a flat baking tray. Place on the floor of the roasting oven, slide the cold shelf onto the second set of runners from the bottom and bake for 12-15 minutes until the filling is set and the pastry golden. Allow to cool. Dust with cocoa and icing sugar and serve.

Serves 6-8.

LEMON MERINGUE ROULADE

....

This roulade looks spectacular, but is simple to make. The actual meringue base can be made up to 5 hours before serving and filled about an hour before needed. Have a large enough tray handy to serve it on.

5 egg whites
5 oz/150g caster sugar
1 tsp cornflour
icing sugar
¹/₂ pint/300ml double cream
6 tbsp lemon curd
2 tsp lemon juice
icing sugar and fruit to decorate

Line the large roasting tin with Bake-O-Glide or non-stick parchment. Whisk the egg whites until white, frothed and doubled in bulk. Whisk in half the sugar and whisk until the mixture is stiff. Continue to whisk the egg white and while doing so, whisk in the remaining sugar and corn-flour 1 teaspoon at a time. Spoon the meringue into the tin and level. Slide the roasting tin onto the bottom set of runners of the roasting oven. Slide the cold shelf onto the runner above. Bake for 10-15 minutes until setting and very pale. Transfer to the simmering oven for a further 40-45 minutes until set. Remove from the oven and cool in the tin.

Lay a sheet of greaseproof paper on the work surface and dust with icing sugar. Whip the cream until softly peaked. Whisk in the lemon curd and lemon juice. Tip the meringue out onto the prepared greaseproof paper. Spread over the cream mixture. Roll up the meringue from one of the short ends. Roll onto a plate. Dust with icing sugar and decorate with fruit.

Serves 6-8.
....

EASTER BISCUITS

Easter Biscuits add to the tea table on Easter Sunday. Currants used to be much prized and were used for special occasions. Sometimes these biscuits were given to children after church on Easter morning, though nowadays I think they prefer chocolate eggs!

4 oz/100g plain white flour
2 oz/50g butter
2 oz/50g caster sugar
1 egg yolk
1/4 tsp ground cinnamon
1 oz/25g currants

Place the butter and sugar in a bowl and cream together until light and fluffy. Beat in the egg yolk with 1 teaspoon of flour. Add the flour, cinnamon and currants and fold into the butter mixture. Flour the work surface lightly and roll the biscuit dough to the thickness of a 50p piece. Cut out rounds and place on a lightly greased baking tray. Bake in the roasting oven with the oven shelf on the bottom set of runners and the cold shelf on the second set of runners from the top. Bake for 10-15 minutes until dry-looking and pale golden brown. Dust with caster sugar and cool on a wire rack.

BAKEWELL SLICES

Bakewell slices are good to serve as a pudding or as cakes. Bake in the roasting tin and cut into portions.

12 oz/350g shortcrust pastry
4 tbsp raspberry jam
2 oz/50g ground almonds
2 oz/50g ground rice
4 oz/100g caster sugar
4 oz/100g butter or margarine
2 eggs
almond essence

Line the small roasting tin with the shortcrust pastry. Spread the jam evenly over the pastry base. Cream together the butter and sugar until light and fluffy. Beat in the eggs, one at a time. Fold in the ground almonds and ground rice. Add 2-3 drops almond essence. Spread the mixture carefully over the prepared pastry case. Bake the tart on the floor of the roasting oven for 20 minutes. If the topping is browning too much but not firm to the touch in the centre, slide in the cold shelf above and cook for a further 10-15 minutes. Remove from the oven. Cool in the tin. Cut into slices and serve.

S I M N E L   C A K E

Traditionally made by girls in service to take home on mid-Lent Sunday, this is now usually made as an Easter cake. This recipe is slightly different to the one in the *Traditional Aga Cookery Book*.

> *6 oz/175g plain flour*
> *2 oz/50g ground almonds*
> *1/2 level tsp baking powder*
> *1/2 tsp grated nutmeg*
> *1/2 tsp mixed spice*
> *grated rind of 1 lemon*
> *6 oz/175g caster sugar*
> *6 oz/175g butter, softened*
> *3 eggs, beaten*
> *7 oz/200g sultanas*
> *7 oz/200g currants*
> *2 oz/50g chopped, mixed peel*
> *apricot jam*
> *1 lb/450g made marzipan*
> *Easter decorations e.g. sugar eggs and chicks for the top*

Line a deep 8"/20cm cake tin and grease well. Take one third of the marzipan and roll it to a circle to fit the tin, then place to one side. Sieve together the flour, ground almonds, baking powder and spices. Add the lemon rind. Cream together the sugar and butter until light and fluffy, and gradually beat in the eggs along with a little flour mixture. Fold in the remaining flour and then the dried fruits. Put half the cake mixture in the prepared tin, lay on the circle of marzipan. Put the remaining cake mixture on top. Level off. The cake may be baked either in the roasting oven, in an Aga cake baker or in an ordinary cake tin in the simmering oven. If using the cake baker, heat the empty outer container in the roasting oven with the oven shelf on the floor of the oven. Place the cake tin in the trivet, place in the cake baker and return to the oven for 1½ hours. The cake should be evenly baked and slightly shrunk from the tin's sides.

If using the simmering oven, place the cake in the oven with the shelf on

the bottom set of runners. Bake for 10-12 hours or overnight, until the cake is an even, golden colour and slightly shrunk from the sides of the tin. For the four-oven Aga put the oven shelf on the floor of the baking oven and bake the cake for 1½-2 hours until the cake is golden brown and slightly shrunk from the sides of the tin. Cool in the tin. Decorate the cake when it is cold. Stand 2 tablespoons apricot jam in a basin on top of the Aga to soften. Take one third of the remaining marzipan and roll a circle to fit the top. Brush the top of the cake with the warmed jam and lay the marzipan circle to fit the top. Press into place. Use the remaining marzipan to make 11 small balls, to represent the Apostles minus Judas. Brush the edge of the marzipan circle with jam and fix on the 11 balls. Decorate the centre with eggs and chicks or fresh Easter flowers.

CHOCOLATE CAKE

A special-occasion cake that, decorated with chocolate flakes and truffles, can look a smart centre-piece for the tea table. Tie a brown tartan ribbon round to make it extra-special.

5 oz/150g self-raising flour
1 oz/25g cocoa
6 oz/175g butter
6 oz/175g soft brown sugar
1 tsp vanilla essence
4 oz/100g plain chocolate, melted
3 tbsp boiling water
4 large eggs

FILLING AND COVERING:
½ pint/300ml double cream
10 oz/275g plain chocolate
chocolates or flake to decorate

Base-line 2 x 9"/24cm cake tins. Sieve the flour and cocoa together. Cream together the butter and sugar. Beat in the melted chocolate mixed with the water. Separate the eggs and beat the yolks into the creamed mixture, folding in a little flour with each yolk. Fold in the remaining flour. Whisk the egg whites until stiff but not dry, and carefully fold into the cake mixture. Divide the mixture between the tins. To bake, put the oven shelf on the floor of the roasting oven, put in the cakes and slide in the cold shelf two runners above. For the four-oven Aga put the shelf on the bottom set of runners in the baking oven. Put the cakes in the oven. Bake for 25-30 minutes until risen, springy and slightly shrunk from the sides of the tin. Turn onto a wire rack and cool.

For the covering, put the chocolate in a bowl to melt on top of the Aga. Pour the cream into a small saucepan, place on the simmering plate and bring to the boil. Pour onto the chocolate and leave to stand, off the Aga, for 5 minutes. Whisk until cold and smooth. Use to fill the cake, sandwich together and use the remaining mixture to cover the top. Decorate.

Makes 12 slices.

BONFIRE NIGHT AND HALLOWE'EN

On dark winter nights, warming food is called for. I can remember having hot baked potatoes round the bonfire on Guy Fawkes night. Nowadays a lot of families go to a large fireworks display, so something warming on return that can be left in the oven is a good idea. Maybe the food will still be eaten outside, around a bonfire, or with a few sparklers, so easy-to-hold food is usually best.

Hallowe'en is a recent celebration, so I have given it an American theme. Cakes can be iced in ghoulish colours e.g. black, orange, lime. Serve with drinks coloured lime and orange. Remember to scoop out the pumpkin carefully and use it to make a lantern as a centrepiece for the table.

DEVILS ON HORSEBACK

I do not know the origin of the name of 'Devils on Horseback', but they sound just right for a Hallowe'en party. Hand them round as nibbles.

12 rashers of streaky bacon
24 prunes
cocktail sticks

Cover the prunes with boiling water and leave to soak overnight. Stretch each rasher of bacon with the back of a table knife and cut in half. Lay the bacon on the rack of the roasting tin and grill for about 5 minutes at the top of the roasting oven. Remove from the oven and wrap a rasher of bacon round each prune, securing the bacon with a cocktail stick or on a skewer. Return to the rack in the tin and cook on the second set of runners from the top of the roasting oven for about 10 minutes until crispy.

Makes 24.

SIZZLING SAUSAGES

Home-made sausages are easy to make. Add some sautéed onions or leeks for a change, or serve with roast onions and baked potatoes.

1 lb/450g minced pork
1 lb/450g minced veal
8 oz/225g shredded suet
8 oz/225g fresh breadcrumbs
1 tbsp chopped fresh herbs or 1 tsp dried mixed herbs
salt and pepper
1 egg, beaten

Mix all the ingredients together well; it is often easiest to do this using your hands. Divide the mixture into about 12 and on a floured work top form into sausage shapes. Stand the rack inside the roasting tin – the small one will take about 8 sausages at a time. Put the sausages on the rack and cook in the roasting oven on the second set of runners from the top. After 20 minutes, turn the sausages and brush them with a little of the fat in the roasting pan. Return to the oven for a further 20 minutes.

Makes 12 sausages.

BAKED POTATOES

Hot baked potatoes warm the hands wonderfully when standing round a bonfire watching fireworks. For easy handling and eating, choose potatoes that are of an even size but not too large. Maincrop varieties are best for this type of cooking. Choose one or two potatoes per person.

FILLINGS:
butter
grated cheese
soured cream and chives
sausages
crispy bacon

Scrub the potatoes and slit the skin on one side – either a long slit to put bacon rashers or sausages in, or a cross. Stand the potatoes directly on the oven shelf and bake on the third runner from the top of the roasting oven. It is difficult to give a time as the size and variety of potato will affect cooking times. Allow at least one hour, and if necessary keep them hot in the simmering oven. Open through the slit and serve with chosen filling.

SPARE RIBS

Spare ribs are ideal for eating with the fingers, and the flavours from this recipe are perfect for eating out of doors. Line the roasting tin with foil or Bake-o-Glide, because the sticky mixture can be difficult to wash off. Only two or three mouthfuls of meat come from each rib, so allow more or less according to what else you are offering. This marinade is sufficient for 4 lbs/2kg pork spare ribs.

4 lb/2kg spare ribs, Chinese style
salt and pepper
4 tbsp clear honey or golden syrup
4 tbsp soft brown sugar
4 tbsp tomato ketchup
2 tbsp Worcester sauce
1 tbsp made mustard
2 tbsp wine vinegar

Mix all the marinade ingredients together. Lay out the ribs in a non-metallic dish. Pour on the marinade and leave for at least 2-3 hours. Place the rack in the lined roasting tin. Lay out the spare ribs. Hang the roasting tin on the highest set of runners of the roasting oven. Roast the spare ribs for 10 minutes then brush on the marinade and continue roasting. Turn and brush on the marinade another time. The ribs will take about 30 minutes to cook and become crispy. Serve.

TACOS

....

I find this 'tex-mex' idea useful for eating in the hand. The small amount of paprika makes the dish warming, and the Taco shells make it easy to pass round. Have some finely shredded cabbage and grated cheese to sprinkle on the top.

1 lb/450g minced beef
large clove garlic, peeled and crushed
1 tsp ground cumin
1 tsp oregano
1-2 tsp paprika, depending upon taste
salt and pepper
14 oz/400g can of tomatoes
14 oz/400g can of kidney beans, drained
box of Taco shells

In a large saucepan, brown the meat on the boiling plate. Add the garlic and all the herbs and spices. Stir well, frying for 1-2 minutes. Blend the tomatoes and beans together until both are chopped but not puréed. Add these to the meat and stir well. Cover and bring to the boil. Transfer to the simmering oven for an hour. The mixture should be thick. Taste and season. Warm the Taco shells in the roasting oven for 4-5 minutes. Allow 2-3 shells per person. Hand round shredded cabbage and grated cheese to top the meat in each shell.

Fills about 12 shells.
....

PUMPKIN PIE

Pumpkins are often cut up for lanterns for Hallowe'en, so why not use the flesh for a pudding? Like marrows, pumpkins have little flavour, so a good flavouring of spice is needed.

8 oz/225g sweet shortcrust pastry
8 oz/225g caster sugar
3 eggs
$1/_3$ pint/200ml milk
$1^1/_2$ tsp ground cinnamon
$1/_2$ tsp ground ginger
$1/_2$ tsp grated nutmeg
the cooked and mashed flesh of 1 medium pumpkin or a 15 oz/425g can of pumpkin flesh

Line an 8"/20cm deep or a 10"/25cm shallow flan ring with the short-crust pastry. Beat together the eggs, sugar, spices and milk. Gradually beat in the pumpkin flesh. Pour into the prepared pastry case. Stand the pie on the floor of the roasting oven and bake for 35-40 minutes until set and golden brown. Serve warm or cold with cream or yoghurt.

Serves 8-10.

BAKED APPLES

Baked apples are appropriate in Autumn. They can be cooked individually or in large quantity for a crowd. They can be filled with dried fruits, mincemeat, even marzipan and cherries. Here, I am using a simple method.

one even-sized apple per person
butter
golden syrup

Core the apple and slit the skin round the circumference of the apple. Place in an ovenproof dish. Put a knob of butter over the hole of each apple. Drizzle about a teaspoonful of golden syrup over each apple. Put a little water in the bottom of the dish. Put the oven shelf on the bottom set of runners of the roasting oven, slide in the dish and bake for 25-40 minutes, depending upon the type and size of apple.

DEVIL'S FOOD CAKE

I am sure this has its name because it is so rich and sinful. The cake is very moist and rich, and the icing, though sweet, gives a lovely contrast in colour and texture. This cake can be kept for a day or two in an airtight tin.

6 oz/175g plain flour
1 level tsp baking powder
$1/_2$ level tsp bicarbonate of soda
2 oz/50g cocoa, mixed with 2-3 tbsp hot water
4 oz/100g butter
8 oz/225g dark soft brown sugar
2 eggs
4 tbsp plain yoghurt

FROSTING:
1 egg white
3 tbsp water, cold
7 oz/200g caster sugar
2 pinches cream of tartar
$1/2$ tsp vanilla essence

Grease and base-line two 8"/20cm sandwich tins. In a large basin put the cake ingredients and mix well until the mixture is light and fluffy and evenly mixed. Divide between the two tins. For the two-oven Aga, place the shelf on the floor of the roasting oven, put in the cakes and slide the cold shelf onto the 3rd set of runners from the top. For the four-oven Aga place the shelf on the bottom set of runners of the baking oven. Bake the cakes for 25-35 minutes until risen, firm to the touch and slightly shrunk from the sides of the tin. Turn onto a cooling rack to cool.

To prepare the frosting, place the egg whites, water, sugar and cream of tartar into a large mixing bowl. Place over a saucepan of simmering water and whisk, preferably with an electric whisk, until white, very stiff and the sugar has dissolved to make a smooth icing. Use some of the icing to spread on one layer of cake, place the second layer on top. Stand the cake on a plate and then spread the remaining icing over the top and sides. Fork over the top to make a rough finish. Allow to set for one hour before slicing.

Cuts into 8-10 slices.

STREUSEL CAKE

The basic idea for this cake came from the Aga Demonstrations handbook. However, my family do not like the mixed peel, so I just put in sultanas. The recipe is sufficient for the small roasting tin.

3 eggs
6 oz/175g self-raising flour
6 oz/175g caster sugar
6 oz/175g softened butter or margarine
grated rind 1 lemon
4 oz/100g sultanas

TOPPING:
4 oz/100g plain flour
2 tspground cinnamon
2 oz/50g soft brown sugar
2 oz/50g demerara sugar
2 oz/50g butter

Line the small roasting tin with Bake-O-Glide or foil. Grease the foil lining. Put the eggs, flour, caster sugar, butter and lemon rind for the cake into a bowl and mix well until light and fluffy. Stir in the sultanas. Put the mixture into the prepared tin and level the top.

Prepare the Streusel topping: measure the flour, cinnamon and sugars into a bowl. Rub in the butter until the mixture resembles breadcrumbs. Sprinkle over the cake mix.

To bake: for the two-oven Aga, slide the roasting tin onto the bottom set of runners of the roasting oven. Put the cold shelf onto the second set of runners from the top. For the four-oven Aga bake the cake on the bottom set of runners of the baking oven. Bake for 40-45 minutes until golden brown, springy to the touch and slightly shrunk from the sides of the tin. Cool on a wire rack. Cut into pieces before serving.

PARKIN

A variation on the gingerbread theme, this is ideal for Bonfire Night, warm and spicy. Like gingerbread, this improves with keeping in a tin for about a week.

4 oz/100g plain flour
4 oz/100g medium oatmeal
1 level tsp bicarbonate of soda
1 level tsp ground ginger
2 oz/50g margarine
4 oz/100g soft brown sugar
4 oz/100g treacle or syrup or mixed
1 egg
3 tbsp milk

Line the small roasting tin with Bake-O-Glide or baking parchment. In a mixing bowl put the margarine, sugar and treacle or syrup. Stand bowl on the Aga until the fat is melted and the sugar mixes in well. Sieve the flour, bicarbonate of soda and ginger together into a mixing bowl. Stir in the oatmeal. Beat together the egg and milk. When the syrup mixture is melted together pour into the flour. Beat in the egg and milk to make a smooth batter. Pour into the prepared tin. For the two-oven Aga hang the roasting tin on the bottom set of runners of the roasting oven. Slide in the cold shelf, two runners above. For the four-oven Aga bake in the baking oven on the bottom set of runners. Bake for 25-30 minutes until risen, slightly shrunk from the sides of the tin and is firm to the touch in the middle. Cool in the tin before cutting into squares.

POPCORN

Children love popcorn – and some adults do too! Make a batch and serve in paper cones to eat round the bonfire or to give for 'trick or treat'.

4 oz/100g popcorn – not the type sold for microwaves
1 tbsp vegetable oil
2 oz/50g butter
6-8 tbsp golden syrup

In a basin put the butter and measure in the golden syrup. Stand it on top of the Aga to melt the butter. In a large, lidded saucepan heat the oil until smoking hot. Quickly tip in the popcorn, put on the lid immediately. Shake the pan and wait until the corn has finished popping. Do not lift the lid before, or the kitchen will be covered in popcorn! Remove from the heat and pour over the syrup and butter mixture. Toss well and serve. Alternatively the corn can be tossed in sea salt or plain sugar.

BREAKFASTS AND BRUNCH

After a party the night before, or when there is a houseful staying, a cooked breakfast can be leisurely. Here the Aga is so good, because fatty smells will not permeate the house.

Serve fruit juices in jugs, maybe fresh grapefruit, toast and marmalade or jam. Croissants can be warmed; I often use the chill/bake variety in a tin. Unroll the dough and shape and bake just before serving. The only problem is that they taste so good you will need a good supply. Bacon, sausages, eggs etc. can be cooked in the oven.

Brunch is very popular, often used for entertaining late morning at weekends. Again fruit juices, tea and coffee, and sometimes Bucks Fizz is appropriate. Home-made bread rolls are delicious as well as toast, soda bread, muffins and croissants. Fluffy pancakes with crispy bacon are unusual. Blinis are good, too. Lightly cooked scrambled eggs, smoked haddock or kippers, or even a thick Spanish omelette are popular.

Some people appreciate something sweet afterwards, so a simple apple cake is good to serve with tea.

B R E A K F A S T S

I give an outline for cooking sausages, bacon, tomato and egg, but of course you can add in any extras such a black pudding, scrambled eggs, mushrooms and kidneys. You will need the roasting tin, so choose the large or small depending upon the quantity you are cooking for. Put into the slightly greased roasting tin the sausages, or the thickest food that takes the most cooking. Slide the tin onto the top set of runners in the roasting oven. Cook the sausages for about 10 minutes until golden brown and sizzling. Remove the tin from the oven and put in the bacon rashers and the tomatoes, cut in half with a cross cut in the middle to help cooking.

Turn the sausages over and return to the oven, again at the top. Cook for a further 10 minutes, this time will depend upon how you like your bacon cooked and the thickness of the rashers. Remove the sausages to a warm plate and into the simmering oven, also the tomato and bacon if cooked to your preference. If not, leave them in the tin. There should be a good smearing of fat from the sausages. Whilst the tin is hot, crack in the eggs and immediately return the pan to the floor of the roasting oven. Cook for 2-3 minutes and, depending on taste, turn the egg over and cook for 1-2 minutes. Serve on warm plates immediately.

Washing-up tip: put the roasting pan to soak in hot soapy water straight away, otherwise the bits of egg can be difficult to clean off.

AGA TOAST

This is a mystery to those who have not used an Aga before and cannot see the grill! The special Aga toaster – like a tennis racket – is needed. Most commercially baked bread is very moist, so to prevent sticking put the toaster under the lid of the boiling plate for about 1 minute to heat up. Remove and place in the bread to toast. Return to the boiling plate. If you like softer toast or are in a hurry, put the lid down, if not keep the lid up. Watch the toast, the time of toasting will vary with the thickness and type of bread and the temperature of your plate. Turn the toast over and do the second side.

P I P E R A D E

This makes a good brunch dish to serve with rashers of back bacon and even triangles of fried bread. The bread can be fried in the roasting tin on the floor of the roasting oven, and the bacon cooked towards the top of the oven on the rack in the small roasting tin. If you are cooking for a lot of people, prepare the pepper and tomato mixture in advance and use as required. Do not over-cook the peppers, they should retain some crunch.

olive oil
6 green peppers, cored, seeded and cut into strips
2 lb/1kg tomatoes, skinned, seeded and roughly chopped
1-2 cloves garlic, skinned and chopped – optional
pinch dried basil
salt and pepper
4 eggs, well beaten

Heat a tablespoonful of oil in a heavy, large frying pan. Add the peppers and stir well. When cooking well, add the tomatoes, garlic, basil and a seasoning of salt and pepper. Stir well and when bubbling, transfer to the floor of the roasting oven for 10-15 minutes until the tomatoes are almost pulp-like. Return to the simmering plate and add the eggs; stir until they begin to thicken. Serve immediately with a rasher of bacon and a triangle of fried bread.

Serves 4.

BAKED EGGS

Serve with fresh toast or warm, home-made bread. For each egg you will need a well buttered small ramekin dish.

1 egg per person
salt and pepper
1 tbsp cream per egg

Stand the buttered ramekins in the roasting tin – the small one will take 6 ramekins. Carefully crack an egg into each ramekin. Season with salt and pepper and spoon some cream over each egg. Pour boiling water into the roasting tin, round the ramekins until the water comes to within $1/_2$"/1cm of the top of the rim. Cover with a sheet of foil and slide into the roasting oven on the bottom set of runners. Bake for 10-12 minutes until the whites are set and the yolks runny – this depends upon the freshness of the egg. Serve immediately.

HERRINGS IN OATMEAL

These are delicious, and of course can be cooked in the Aga without smelling out the whole house. A good fishmonger will remove most of the bones and the heads from the herrings for you. Serve with good wholemeal bread.

4 herrings
salt and pepper
fine oatmeal
2 oz/50g butter
1 lemon

Clean the flesh of the fish by rubbing with a little salt and rinse off. Dry well on kitchen paper. Toss the fish in salt and pepper and coat well with the fine oatmeal, pressing it on well. Put the butter in a strong frying pan, or the roasting tin if cooking in the roasting oven. Melt the butter and fry the fish until golden brown. Turn it over and do the second side – about 5 minutes per side depending on the thickness of the fish. Cut the lemon into wedges. Serve the drained fish with lemon wedges on warm plates.

Serves 4.

HOT BREAKFAST FRUITS

Warm croissants and fruit make a delicious alternative to the usual breakfast, and a very healthy one. The fruit is equally nice at room temperature.

4 oz/100g prunes
6 oz/175g dried apricots
3 bananas
3 tbsp honey
grated rind and juice of 1 lemon
6 tbsp orange juice

Place the prunes and apricots in a basin. Cover with boiling water and allow to stand for several hours or overnight, until plumped up. Stone the prunes and lay them in an oven-proof dish with the apricots and the bananas cut into chunks. Drizzle over the honey, add the lemon juice and rind and toss the fruit. Pour over the orange juice. Cover with a lid or foil. For the two-oven Aga put the shelf on the floor of the roasting oven and cook the fruit for 20 minutes. For the four-oven Aga put the shelf on the second set of runners from the top of the baking oven. Cook the fruit for about 30 minutes. Serve.

Serves 6

CINNAMON TOAST

This is traditionally a winter tea-time treat, but I like it for breakfast or brunch.

4 slices of bread, not too thick
1 tsp ground cinnamon
2 tbsp caster sugar
butter for spreading

Mix together the sugar and cinnamon. Have the oven shelf on the highest runner possible in the roasting oven. Toast the bread on one side only, either with the toast 'bat' on the boiling plate or put the bread directly on the simmering plate. Remove the toast and thickly butter the un-toasted side. Sprinkle on the sugar and spice mixture. Place on a baking sheet, spice side uppermost. Slide onto the shelf in the roasting oven and cook until the mixture starts to melt. Cut the toast into fingers and serve.

BRAN MUFFINS

Delicious for breakfast, bran muffins are both healthy and quick to make. Serve warm with butter, honey or marmalade.

4 oz/100g plain wholemeal flour
2 level tsp baking powder
1 level tsp salt
2 oz/50g natural bran
2 good tbsp wheatgerm
1½ oz/35g caster sugar
1 egg
½ pint/300ml milk
4 tbsp vegetable oil

Brush a twelve-bun tin with oil. Place the flour, baking powder, salt, bran, wheatgerm and sugar in a mixing bowl. Mix together the egg, milk and oil. Add to the flour mixture and stir in just enough to mix together. Divide the muffin mix between the 12 bun moulds. Place the oven shelf on the third set of runners from the top of the roasting oven. Slide in the muffins and bake for 25-30 minutes until they are risen and golden brown. Serve warm.

Makes 12.

BLUEBERRY AND WALNUT MUFFINS

Muffins are quick and easy to make, but they must be eaten when freshly made. Serve with butter for breakfast.

8 oz/225g plain flour
4 oz/100g caster sugar
2 tsp baking powder
1 oz/25g chopped walnuts
5 fl oz/150ml milk
3 fl oz/100ml cooking oil
1 egg
4 oz/100g blueberries

Wash the blueberries and stew to soften in a scant tablespoon water. Set aside when softened. Measure into a large mixing bowl the flour, sugar, baking powder and walnuts. Mix together. Beat together the egg, milk and oil. Stir the egg mixture into the dry ingredients. Fold in the cooked blueberries. Take care not to over-mix. Divide the mixture between 9 deep lined muffin tins or 12 lined bun tins. Put the shelf on the third set of runners from the top in the roasting oven. Slide in the muffin tins and bake for 10-15 minutes until risen and golden brown.

Makes 9 large or 12 small muffins.

SODA BREAD

Soda Bread comes from Ireland and is a quick bread to make for breakfast or at the last minute when unexpected guests arrive. It is also good served with cheese for lunch.

1 lb/450g plain wholemeal flour
4 oz/100g plain flour
1 tsp bicarbonate of soda
1 tsp salt
about 15 fl oz/450ml buttermilk or plain yoghurt

Put the flours, bicarbonate of soda and salt in a mixing bowl. Add enough buttermilk or yoghurt to make a soft dough. Knead lightly on a floured work top. Shape into a large round about the thickness of your hand and place on a greased baking sheet. Cut a deep cross in the top. Bake on the second set of runners down from the top of the roasting oven for 10 minutes then move the shelf to the bottom set of runners for the next 30 minutes until the loaf sounds hollow when tapped on the bottom. Serve warm.

CHRISTENINGS AND
FAMILY CELEBRATIONS

Traditionally, babies were christened in the afternoon and tea and cakes were offered to the guests afterwards. In recent years there has been a change of emphasis, and most babies are christened during the morning service, so lunch is usually offered to family and friends.

With a small baby to keep calm, a little advance preparation is vital, so that there is not too much rushing around in the morning. Have some nibbles and drinks ready so the host and hostess have time for last-minute preparations after the return from church.

I have suggested cold dishes, but of course if the Christening is in winter, a rich warming casserole can be in the oven before leaving for church.

A cake is lovely with a glass of sparkling wine to toast the baby's future. A rich fruit cake beautifully decorated is traditional, but I give here the recipe for a light textured golden cake with a soft lemony frosting. Decorate with sugared fruit or traditional Christening decorations.

COLD BEEF STROGANOFF

I have made this recipe so many times for buffet lunches and smart picnics. It makes a good alternative to cold beef. Although the beef is fillet or sirloin and fairly expensive, it does seem to go a long way.

1 1/2 lb/675g fillet or sirloin of beef
flour to coat
salt and pepper
4 oz/100g butter
8 oz/225g button mushrooms, wiped and sliced
8 oz/225g onion, diced
2 tbsp lemon juice
1/2 pint/300ml tomato juice
1 tsp made mustard
5 fl oz/150ml double cream, whipped lightly
1/2 pint/300ml soured cream or crème fraîche
chopped chives to garnish

Cut the beef into matchstick strips. Toss in seasoned flour. Melt half the butter in a large frying pan and fry the beef, in batches, over a high heat for about 5 minutes until browned well and cooked through. When cooked, put the meat in a bowl. Melt the remaining butter in the frying pan on the simmering plate and fry the mushrooms until cooked. Remove with a slotted spoon and add to the meat. Add the onion to the frying pan and cook until clear and softened – do not brown. Add to the meat. Mix together the lemon juice, mustard and tomato juice. Pour over the meat and stir well. Cover and chill well. Fold the cream and half the soured cream together. Stir into the chilled meat mixture. Season to taste. Put the Stroganoff onto a serving dish and garnish with the remaining soured cream and sprinkle with chopped chives.

Serves 10-12.

GRILLED SALMON STEAKS WITH CUCUMBER PICKLE

....

Salmon is easy to cook, but it often needs a sauce or dressing to add flavour or to make it different. Serve this salmon warm or cold as part of a buffet lunch or as a starter.

5 fl oz/150ml white wine vinegar
2 oz/50g caster sugar
1 oz/25g mustard seeds, lightly crushed
1 small onion, finely chopped
1/2 small cucumber, finely sliced
1 tsp cornflour
10 small, thin salmon steaks
2-3 tbsp olive oil
salt and pepper

To make the pickle, place the wine vinegar, caster sugar, mustard seeds and onion into a small saucepan. Stand the pan on the simmering plate and stir until the sugar has dissolved. Continue to cook over a gentle heat until the onion is soft. Add the cucumber and continue to cook for 1-2 minutes to soften the cucumber. Blend the cornflour with a little water. Stir into the cucumber mixture and cook, stirring until thickening. Transfer to a bowl and cool.

Place the cleaned salmon steaks on the rack of the roasting tin. Brush lightly with olive oil and season. Slide the roasting tin onto the second set of runners from the top of the roasting oven. Grill the salmon for 7-10 minutes, depending upon thickness. Turn the salmon over, brush with olive oil and season. Repeat the grilling. Remove from the oven. Remove any skin from the salmon, this is easier to do after cooking. Serve the salmon warm or cold with the cucumber pickle.

....

CHILLED LEMON CHICKEN

Coronation chicken is always popular, but for a change I like the delicate flavour of this lemon chicken to serve for a cold buffet dish. The recipe is enough for six, but larger chickens can be used, or even two or three chickens cooked at a time, if catering for a crowd. Serve with fragrant Thai rice and a colourful salad.

3¹/₂-4 lb/1.5-1.75kg chicken
1 onion
2-3 bay leaves
salt and pepper

FOR THE SAUCE:
1 oz/25g butter
1 oz/25g flour
¹/₂ pint/300ml chicken liquor
salt and pepper
1 lemon, juice and finely grated rind
2 egg yolks
¹/₂ pint/300ml single cream

Place the chicken in a large saucepan. Put in the peeled whole onion, the bay leaves and some salt and pepper. Cover with cold water. Put on the lid and stand the pan on the simmering plate or on the floor of the roasting oven. Bring slowly to the boil (this can take up to 1 hour). When boiling, transfer to the simmering oven and cook for a further 1-1¹/₂ hours, depending on the size of the chicken. Remove from the oven and allow the chicken to cool in the liquor. When cool, remove the chicken. Discard the skin and bones and chop the flesh into even-sized chunks.

To prepare the lemon sauce, skim the fat from the liquor and measure it into a saucepan. Add the butter and flour and stand it over a medium heat and whisk all the time until a thickened sauce is made. Simmer for 1-2 minutes. Add the lemon juice and rind. In a basin mix the egg yolks and

cream, add to the hot sauce and whisk well. Cook, whisking all the time, over the simmering plate for 1-2 minutes. DO NOT ALLOW TO BOIL. Remove from the heat, check seasoning, then pour into a bowl and allow to cool. When cold, fold in the prepared chicken. Chill and allow the flavours to mingle. Serve on a bed of rice.

VEGETABLE COUSCOUS

Couscous is a wonderful alternative to rice and pasta. It is so easy to prepare and can be served hot or cold. Often it is served as a salad with chopped tomatoes, cucumber, mint and salad dressing. This recipe is served warm.

1 lb/450g couscous
8 oz/225g broccoli florets
4 oz/100g peas
4 oz/100g mange-tout peas
4 spring onions
juice of 1 lemon
8 tbsp olive oil
1 tsp mustard
salt and pepper

Place the couscous in a mixing bowl and cover with boiling water. Cover the bowl with a plate and leave to stand while preparing the other ingredients. Trim the broccoli florets and top and tail the mange-tout. Bring a pan of water to the boil, add a pinch of salt, the broccoli and mange-tout, return to the boil and then add the peas. Boil for 2 minutes and then drain the vegetables. Drain the couscous of any liquid, gently stir in the broccoli, mange-tout and peas. Finely slice the trimmed spring onions, add to the couscous mixture. Whisk together the lemon juice, olive oil, mustard and salt and pepper to taste. Pour over the couscous. Serve warm.

Serves 8.

THE AGA CHEESECAKE

This recipe came originally from an old Aga calendar. I have made this recipe many times and I am always being asked for the recipe. It is a large cheesecake so you will need a 10"/25cm spring-release or loose-bottomed tin. Top with fresh fruit, or you could use a packet of mixed summer berries from the freezer. This is useful if the filling splits in the middle, which I find often happens. You can freeze this for 1 month.

1 lb/450g digestive biscuits, crumbed
6 oz/175g butter, melted
2 lb/1kg curd cheese
6 oz/175g caster sugar
2 eggs, beaten
1 tsp vanilla essence
2 tbsp cornflour
large carton thick-set or Greek-style plain yoghurt
fresh fruit or fruit compote to decorate

Mix the biscuit crumbs and the melted butter together well. Press firmly into the base of a 10"/26cm spring-release deep cake tin. Chill well in the freezer. In a bowl beat together the curd cheese and the sugar until creamy. Beat in the eggs, vanilla essence and cornflour. Fold in the yoghurt. Pour onto the chilled biscuit crust and bake. Put the shelf on the floor of the roasting oven, slide in the tin and bake for 7 minutes or until the filling is set. Remove from the oven and make a tent of foil over the cheesecake, tucked around the tin. Put the shelf on the floor of the sim-mering oven, slide in the tented cheesecake and bake for about 6 hours. Remove from the oven and chill before decorating and serving.

Serves 12.

BAKED STUFFED PEACHES

....

Baking brings out the lovely summery flavour of the peaches even when they are slightly under ripe. I use this recipe for those peaches that will not ripen, just rot. Serve with cream or Greek-style yoghurt. It is easy to increase the quantities for a crowd – fill the large roasting tin, prepare in advance and bake as needed.

4 large peaches or nectarines
2 level dsp caster sugar
1 oz/25g unsalted butter, softened
1 egg yolk
2 oz/50g Amaretti biscuits, finely crushed

Halve the peaches and remove stones. Arrange in an oven-proof dish, cut side up. Cream together the sugar and butter until light and fluffy. Beat in the egg yolk. Work in the crushed Amaretti biscuits. Pile the stuffing into the peach halves. Bake in the 2-oven Aga with the shelf on the floor of the oven. For the four-oven Aga, have the shelf on the second set of runners from the top in the baking oven. Bake for 20-30 minutes, depending upon the ripeness of the fruit, until the peaches are soft but still holding their shape. Serve warm.

....
Serves 4.
....

LEMON FROSTED CAKE

Make this cake simply just with buttercream icing and a dusting of icing sugar, or ice with a soft frosting with, in this case, a lemon flavour. This can be made and iced up to 5 days before it is needed.

CAKE:
8 oz/225g self-raising flour
2 level tsp baking powder
8 oz/225g caster sugar
8 oz/225g soft margarine
4 eggs
1 tsp vanilla essence

BUTTERCREAM FILLING:
4 oz/175g butter, softened
8 oz/225g icing sugar, sieved
2 tbsp lemon juice
8 dried apricots, ready-to-eat variety, chopped

Grease and base line an 8"/20cm round, deep cake tin. If using the cake baker, put this in the oven to heat up. Place all the cake ingredients in a mixing bowl and beat well until light and fluffy. Place in the prepared tin and level the top. If using the cake baker, put the cake in and cook in the roasting oven with the shelf on the floor of the oven. Bake for approximately 50 minutes.

Alternatively for the two-oven Aga, put the shelf on the floor of the roasting oven, put in the cake and slide the cold shelf above the tin, allowing room for the cake to rise. Time for 30 minutes then carefully make a dome of foil over the cake tin – you may need to put the cold shelf higher, and bake for another 20-30 minutes. For the four-oven Aga bake the cake in the baking oven, with the shelf on the bottom set of runners for 50-60 minutes. The cake should be risen, golden brown, shrunk from the side of the tin and cooked in the middle when tested with a skewer. Remove from the tin and cool completely.

For the filling, cream the butter until soft and fluffy, and gradually beat in the icing sugar and lemon juice. Fold in the chopped apricots. Split the cake horizontally into 3 layers. Divide the buttercream between two portions, spread over evenly and re-assemble the cake. Either dust with icing sugar or marzipan and icing.

1 lb/450g box marzipan
2 tbsp sieved apricot jam, warmed
12 oz/350g icing sugar, sieved
2 fl oz/50ml lemon juice
1 oz/25g caster sugar

Brush the cake all over with the warmed apricot jam. Roll out the marzipan; roll one third to a circle to fit the top. Roll out the remaining two thirds to a strip to fit the sides of the cake. Lay the top piece on and press down. Gently wrap the strip round the side, press on and trim. The cake can be left for 24 hours uncovered before icing if convenient. Stand it on a serving plate or board.

For the icing, place the icing sugar in a large bowl. Put the lemon juice and caster sugar in a small saucepan. Heat gently and allow the sugar to dissolve, then bring to the boil and pour into the icing sugar, beating well. When smooth, use to ice the top and sides of the cake immediately. Allow to stand for 24 hours to allow the icing to harden before decorating and serving.

COFFEE ECLAIRS

Eclairs are just right for afternoon tea. They can be made small and finger-sized, or for less delicate appetites, long and full of cream. Coffee is less sweet than chocolate icing, but melted chocolate can be used if preferred.

2¹/₂ oz/65g plain flour
2 oz/50g butter
2 eggs beaten
5 fl oz/150ml cold water

FILLING:
¹/₂ pint/300ml double cream

ICING:
6 oz/175g icing sugar, sieved
2 tsp instant coffee
1 tbsp boiling water

Put the water and butter in a saucepan and place on the simmering plate to melt the butter and then to boil. Meanwhile, sieve the flour onto a plate. When the butter-water mixture is boiling, tip in the flour all at once and beat well with a wooden spoon. When the mixture leaves the sides of the pan clean, remove from the heat. Beat in the eggs – an electric whisk is easiest. Put the choux paste into a piping bag with a plain nozzle. Grease two baking trays and pipe the paste into 4"/10cm lengths. Space them well to allow for rising. Put the shelf on the bottom set of runners in the roasting oven. Slide in the trays and bake the eclairs for about 20 minutes until risen, golden brown and crisp. Turn the eclairs onto a cooling rack and slit each one down one side to allow steam to escape. Cool.

Whip the cream and put into a piping bag. Prepare the icing: dissolve the coffee in the boiling water. Sieve in the icing sugar and stir well. The icing should be the thickness of thick cream. Pipe the cream into the eclairs. Dip the tops of the eclairs into the coffee icing. Allow to set before serving. This will make about 8 eclairs, depending upon the size chosen.

CHOCOLATE BROWNIES

Chocolate brownies traditionally have a crusty top, but for ease of slicing for a large crowd, these still have the flavour and moistness, but a less crispy top. Double the ingredients to fill the large roasting tin.

4 oz/100g cream cheese
3 oz/75g plain chocolate, melted
8 oz/225g soft brown sugar
4 oz/100g soft margarine
4 oz/100g self-raising flour
1 tbsp cocoa powder
1/2 tsp vanilla essence
3 eggs

Line the small roasting tin either with Bake-O-Glide or foil. Sieve together the flour and cocoa powder in a mixing bowl. Add the eggs, margarine, sugar and cream cheese. Beat the ingredients together to make a smooth mixture. Add the melted chocolate and vanilla essence and beat well. Pour the mixture into the prepared roasting tin. For the two-oven Aga, hang the tin on the bottom set of runners of the roasting oven. Slide the cold shelf onto the third set of runners from the top in the baking oven. For the four-oven Aga, slide the tin onto the third set of runners from the top. Bake for approximately 30 minutes until risen, springy to the touch and slightly shrunk from the sides of the tin. Cool on a wire rack. Cut into squares.

ENTERTAINING

N I B B L E S

....

Make a selection of nibbles to hand around at a drinks party or before a dinner party. A lot of recipes can be adapted and just made smaller such as scones. Hand them round on a large platter or tray with a variety of each nibble. Put on some cherry tomatoes, olives and nuts in small bowls as well.

S A L M O N   S A M O S A S

....

Little samosas are tasty for starters, nibbles and picnics. This method is easy because they are baked in the oven and not deep-fried. If making the day before, refresh the pastry in the roasting oven for 5 minutes.

1 shallot, peeled and finely chopped
1 tbsp vegetable oil
¹/₂ cucumber, diced
8 oz/225g salmon, cooked and flaked
salt and pepper
2 tbsp cream
1 tsp dill, finely chopped
1 tsp chives, finely chopped
6 sheets filo pastry
2 oz/50g butter, melted
sesame or poppy seeds

Put the oil in a small saucepan and heat gently. Add the onion and cook slowly until transparent. Add the diced cucumber and cook for a further 2 minutes. Remove from the heat and mix in the salmon, salt and pepper, cream and herbs. Set aside to cool.

Cut the sheets of filo pastry into 1¹/₂"/4cm wide strips. Brush a strip of pastry with melted butter. Place a teaspoonful of salmon mixture on the

bottom corner. Fold over into a triangle and continue to fold over again and again until the end of the filo strip is reached and a tight triangle parcel has been formed. Place on a baking sheet. Use up all the mixture and then brush with melted butter and sprinkle lightly with poppy or sesame seeds.

Bake on the third set of runners from the top of the roasting oven for 10-15 minutes until puffed up and golden brown.

OTHER FILLING SUGGESTIONS:
finely chopped stir-fry vegetables
cream cheese and spinach
chicken curry
rice and prawns

Makes about 24.

FILO TARTS

Make these in small 1½"/4cm diameter bun/muffin tins.

filo pastry
melted butter

Unwrap the filo pastry and cut some squares. The most economical size will depend upon your type of filo, but approximately 3"/7.5cm square. Re-cover the stack of filo pastry not being used in order to prevent drying out. Brush melted butter on the first sheet of filo. Lay a second square on top at an angle to form a star shape, and brush with butter. Lay on a third square, again at an angle so that all 12 points are showing. Lift and gently ease into a well-buttered muffin tin. Press into the shape of the tin and have the excess pastry edges standing upright. When the tray is complete, bake on the floor of the roasting tin for 8-10 minutes until golden brown and cooked through. Allow to stand for a few minutes before removing

each case to a cooling rack. Fill as required.

FILLING IDEAS:
1 tsp hollandaise sauce topped with thin slivers of smoked salmon
cream cheese topped with half a strawberry
smoked mackerel pâté softened with a little Greek yoghurt, topped with a tiny parsley sprig

MINI SAVOURY SCONES

Make up a batch of scone mix. Before adding the liquid, divide the mixture in half and flavour each separately. The scones are then made small by cutting with a small round cocktail or sweet cutter. When cooked, split in half and spread on some cream cheese, plain or herbed. Garnish with herbs, asparagus tips, slivers of ham or cooked fish.

8 oz/225g self-raising flour
1 oz/25g butter
pinch salt
$1/_4$-$1/_2$ pint/150-300ml milk
either 1 tbsp chopped mixed herbs
or 1 tbsp chopped sun-dried tomatoes

Sieve flour and salt. Rub in the butter. Divide in two and stir in either herbs or sun-dried tomatoes. Stir in $1/_4$ pint/150ml milk, using a knife to make a soft but not sticky dough. Use extra milk if needed. Turn the dough onto a lightly floured work surface – treat lightly. Press down with the palm of your hand until the dough is the thickness of your hand. Stamp out with the cutter. Place on a baking tray. Put the shelf on the third set of runners from the top of the roasting oven, slide in the baking tray. Bake for 10 minutes until risen, dry and firm to the touch. Allow to cool before splitting and spreading with filling.

BEEF SATAY STICKS

Make these on cocktail sticks and serve on a platter with a bowl of dipping sauce. You can also marinade strips of chicken and serve alongside the beef.

4 oz/100g rump steak
1 tsp ground coriander
1 tbsp mild curry powder
4 tbsp coconut milk

SAUCE:
4 oz/100g peanuts, roughly chopped
1 tbsp soft brown sugar
1 tsp hot chilli sauce
8 fl oz/225ml coconut milk

Trim the meat of any excess fat and slice into thin strips. Mix the coriander, curry powder and coconut milk together, stir in the meat, cover and allow to stand for 4 hours or overnight.

To make the sauce, combine the sauce ingredients in a small saucepan. Stand it on the simmering plate and bring to the boil, stirring. When simmering, transfer the pan to the floor of the roasting oven and allow it to simmer for 15 minutes. Remove and pass through a food processor or liquidiser. The sauce should be thick. Pour into a dish and allow to cool.

Thread the meat onto cocktail sticks, about 30-40, and put them on the rack in the roasting tin. Cover the stick ends with a sheet of foil. Slide the tin onto the second set of runners from the top of the roasting oven and cook for 5 minutes. Turn over the sticks and cook for a further 5 minutes until cooked. Serve warm or cold.

GOAT'S CHEESE CROUSTADE

To make small, bite-size rounds choose a small, thin French stick.

¹/₂ thin French stick
olive oil
about 4 oz/100g soft rindless goat's cheese
chives

Slice the bread into thin, mouth-size rounds. Put them on the simmering plate and toast until golden brown. Turn over to toast on the reverse side. When toasted, place on a baking tray. Drizzle olive oil over them. Lay on a slice of goat's cheese. Garnish with strips of fresh chives.

COCKTAIL SAUSAGES

Buy small, good quality cocktail sausages and serve on cocktail sticks.

cocktail sausages
thin rashers streaky bacon – half as many as sausages
tomato ketchup or barbecue sauce

De-rind and stretch each rasher of bacon with the back of a table knife. Cut each rasher into four. Cut each sausage in half and wrap with a rasher of bacon. Skewer with a cocktail stick. Brush each with either tomato ketchup or barbecue sauce – you may find it easier to 'let-down' the sauce with a drop of vinegar and water. Lay the sausages onto a baking tray or the grill rack if they will not fall through! Cover the stick ends with foil. Cook the sausages on the second set of runners from the top of the roasting oven for 5 minutes, turn and cook for another 5 minutes until the bacon is crisp. Serve hot.

MINI EMMENTAL AND GRUYÈRE TARTLETS

Make these very small, if you have little tart tins, if not, make a larger tart and cut into small squares. The cheeses melt well to make a rich tasty tart. Do not use salt, as Swiss cheese has a saltiness of its own when cooked.

2 oz/50g Emmental, grated finely
2 oz/50g Gruyère, grated finely
2 eggs
$^1/_2$ pint/300ml single cream
pepper
6 oz/175g shortcrust pastry

Use the shortcrust pastry to line the tart tins. Mix the cheeses and divide between the lined tart tins. Beat the eggs, cream and pepper together. Pour a little egg mixture over the cheese so that the tart is three-quarters full. Put the tray on the floor of the roasting oven and bake for 15-20 minutes until the pastry is crisp and the filling is risen and golden.

Makes 24 mini-tarts.

MINI-CROISSANTS

I find the best way to make these is to buy the tin of mini-baguette dough from the chill counter of the supermarket.

1 tin x 4 baguette mix chilled dough
4 oz/100g Gruyère, cut into thin slices
1 egg, beaten for glazing

Unroll the dough and cut each baguette shape into 4 triangles. Lay onto each triangle a slice of Gruyère. Roll each triangle from the wide end to the point to form a mini-croissant. Space them out on the greased cold shelf. Brush each croissant with beaten egg. Bake on the third set of runners from the top of the roasting oven for about 10 minutes until puffed up and golden brown. Serve warm.

DINNER PARTY DISHES

....

GINGERED POUSSINS

....

Poussins are now readily available from butchers and supermarkets. This recipe gives lots of flavours and looks attractive. The recipe given is for 6, but it can be easily multiplied for a crowd as everything is cooked in the oven. Serve thick, wholemeal bread to mop up the juices and a crisp salad afterwards.

6 lemons
2 inch/5cm piece fresh root ginger
8 tbsp runny honey
4 fl oz/150ml vegetable oil
salt and pepper
3 poussins, halved
1 lb/450g onions, peeled and sliced
1 1/2 oz/35g soft brown sugar

Whisk together the grated rind and juice of 5 lemons, the peeled and grated root ginger, honey, vegetable oil and salt and pepper. Put the poussins into a non-metallic dish and pour over the marinade mixture. Cover and chill for 12 hours or overnight.

Remove the poussins from the marinade and place in the roasting tin. Pour over half the marinade. Slide the roasting tin onto the second set of runners of the roasting oven and roast the meat for about 45 minutes, basting occasionally.

Pour the remaining marinade into a saucepan with the onions and sugar. Stand the pan on the simmering plate and bring to the boil. When boiling, stir and then transfer to the simmering oven. Cook for 40-45 minutes until the onions have caramelised. Put the poussins on a warm plate and

keep warm. Bubble juices on the simmering plate until reduced. Put a bed of caramelised onions on each plate, top with a halved poussin, pour over the remaining juices. Serve with a slice of the remaining lemon.

Serves 6.

SALMON EN CROÛTE

Serve this piping hot on a buffet table for a lunch party. The variety of layers look attractive when sliced through. A very sharp knife is essential when slicing. Prepare in advance, chill and bake as needed.

3¹/₂-4 lb/1.6-2kg salmon or sea trout, cleaned, skinned and
filleted – about 2 lb/1kg finished weight
1 orange
1 level tsp ground black pepper
1 tbsp chopped dill
1¹/₂ lb/750g ready-made puff pastry
12 oz/350g frozen chopped spinach, thawed
4 oz/100g low fat soft cheese
salt and pepper
4 oz/100g spring onions, chopped
1 oz/25g butter
4 oz/100g cooked, peeled prawns
1 egg, beaten

Put the two prepared fish fillets together and place in a non-metallic dish. Grate the orange rind and reserve. Squeeze the juice and mix together with the pepper and dill. Rub into the salmon flesh. Cover and leave to marinate for at least an hour. Roll out half the pastry to a rectangle 15" x 8"/38 x 20.5cm. Place on a baking sheet and prick all over with a fork. Bake in the middle of the roasting oven for about 15 minutes until golden and cooked through. Cool on a wire rack. Squeeze the excess liquid from the spinach and beat into the cheese. Melt the butter in a small pan and cook the onions, but do not brown. Add the prawns and orange rind.

Season to taste.

Return the cooked pastry to a baking sheet, and place one salmon fillet on it. Trim the pastry allowing $1/_2$"/1cm all round the fish. Spread the spinach mixture over the fish. Spoon over the prepared prawn mixture. Finish with the remaining fish fillet. Brush the pastry edge with beaten egg. Roll out the remaining pastry and place over the fish. Trim off most of the excess pastry and reserve. Tuck in 1"/2.5cm all round the fish.

Decorate with a thin lattice cut from the trimmings. Brush all over with beaten egg. Make two small air holes in the top. Put the oven shelf on the middle set of runners in the roasting oven. Bake for 40-45 minutes until risen and golden brown. Serve warm.

Serves 8-10.

RICH CASSEROLE OF HARE

Hare is a rich meat and lends itself well to rich, warming casseroles cooked slowly. This recipe serves 4, but it can easily be increased. Serve with creamy, mashed potatoes and simple vegetables. Prepared portions of hare are now available from many of the supermarket chains.

4 hare portions
bouquet garni e.g. thyme, sage, marjoram
5 fl oz/150ml rich, red wine
2 onions, peeled and sliced
1 oz/25g plain flour
2 oz/50g butter
1 tsp made mustard
5 fl oz/150ml beef stock

Put the hare portions in a non-metallic dish. Season with salt and pepper, pour on the wine and bury the bouquet garni in the centre. Cover and leave to marinate for 2-3 hours. Melt the butter in a frying pan. Cook the onion until softened, but not browned. Transfer to a casserole dish. Toss the drained hare joints in the flour and brown well in the remaining melted butter. Transfer it to the casserole. Pour the remaining marinade, stock and mustard into the pan juices, bring to the boil, stirring. Pour over the meat. Bring the entire casserole to the boil and then transfer to the simmering oven for 2-2½ hours until the meat is tender. Place the meat on a plate and keep warm. Boil the juices to make a thick sauce. Pour over the meat.

Serves 4.

PIZZAIOLA STEAK

A lovely summer dish to eat when tomatoes and fresh basil are plentiful and full of flavour. If you do not have the ridged Aga grill pan, a good quality frying pan can be used. Crusty bread is good for mopping up the juices.

4 thin cut rump steaks
2 cloves garlic, skinned and crushed
salt and pepper
1 lb/450g tomatoes, skinned and chopped
2 tbsp chopped fresh basil
2 tbsp chopped fresh parsley
olive oil

Heat the Aga grill pan on the floor of the roasting oven for 3-4 minutes until really hot. Place in the steaks and fry quickly for 2-3 minutes until browned both sides. Add the garlic, salt and pepper. Add the tomatoes and herbs and a little olive oil if necessary. Cook for 3-5 minutes until the tomatoes are softened. Serve immediately.

Serves 4.

ROAST RACK OF PORK WITH ROAST APPLES

A roast is an easy meal to prepare for about 10 people. This dish uses a whole loin of pork, now often called a rack. Have the butcher prepare the meat so that carving is easy. The chine bone is best removed.

6 lb/3kg loin or rack of pork
a little oil
coarse sea salt
1 eating apple per person
1 tbsp cornflour
1/2 pint/300ml apple juice
1/2 pint/300ml light stock

Twist pieces of foil round any exposed bones to prevent burning. Score the skin well. Lightly brush the skin with oil. Rub in coarse sea salt. Place the meat in the large roasting tin. Roast towards the top (as high as it will go) of the roasting oven for 20 minutes. Move to the bottom set of runners for 1 1/4 hours. Core the apples. Cut in half. Lay around the meat, cut side up. Drizzle over a little oil or baste with meat fat. Return to the oven and roast for a further 1/4-1/2 hour until all is well cooked. Remove the foil from the bones. Allow the meat to rest in a warm place while making the apple gravy. Blend the cornflour and the apple juice. Add either some meat juices or stock. Bring to the boil in a small pan until a thin, light gravy is formed. Carve the meat, cutting between each pair of ribs. Serve with the roast apples and apple gravy.

Serves 8-10.

MONKFISH STIR-FRY

A slightly fiery stir-fry, but it can be toned-down by using less Tabasco sauce. This dish is good for a quick lunch. Have all the ingredients ready before starting to cook.

12 oz/350g monkfish – or other firm, white fish, skinned and
trimmed
juice of 1 lemon
2 tbsp hot red pepper oil or a few shakes Tabasco and 2 tbsp
olive oil
1 tbsp tomato purée
8 spring onions, trimmed and sliced
1 red pepper, de-seeded and sliced finely
8 oz/225g baby corn
green noodles or rice to serve

Wash the fish and pat dry on kitchen paper. Trim into 1"/2.5cm cubes. In a bowl mix together the lemon juice, tomato purée and the hot red pepper oil. Toss in the fish, mix well, cover. Leave to marinade for 2-3 hours in the fridge. Heat a wok or large frying pan. Stir in the fish, lightly drained. Stir well and add the onions, pepper and corn. Keep stirring for 1-2 minutes until cooked. Add the remaining marinade and heat through.

Serves 6.

FILET DE BOEUF EN CROÛTE

Although this is a classic French recipe, it is best made with good English beef. The fillet of beef is the best cut, and ask the butcher for a good even shape, preferably from the thick end. If you want to cook for more than eight, it is easier to use two separate fillets and cook them individually than one enormously long fillet.

3 lb/1.5kg fillet of beef in the piece
2 oz/50g butter
salt and pepper
4 oz/100g mushrooms
1 tbsp chopped fresh herbs
8 oz/225g packet puff pastry
beaten egg for glazing

If the skin is still on the fillet, score it with a sharp knife. Melt the butter in the small roasting tin on the floor of the roasting oven. Season the meat and then roll in the melted butter to coat all over. Hang the roasting tin on the third set of runners from the top of the roasting oven and roast the meat for 20 minutes – a little less for rare joints, approximately 10 minutes more for a more well-done finished joint. Remove the meat to a plate and allow to cool. Wash and slice the mushrooms, toss them in the roasting pan and add the herbs. Put the pan on the floor of the roasting oven and cook the mushrooms until just cooked, about 8-10 minutes. Remove and cool.

Roll the pastry to 1"/2.5cm longer than the fillet and three times as wide. Cut off two thirds from the width. Spoon the mushrooms down the centre of the larger piece. Lay the fillet on top. Bring the pastry up the sides of the meat, pressing to secure in place. Fold the ends up neatly. Gently transfer to a baking tray or the washed roasting tin. Roll the remaining pastry to make it slightly longer. Brush the sides of the fillet pastry with egg, gently lift on the rolled strip of pastry. Seal against the pastry already on the meat. Decorate with leaves made from any trimmings. Brush the

pastry all over with beaten egg. Chill.

When ready to cook, put the oven shelf on the third set of runners from the top of the roasting oven. Slide in the meat and cook for 35 minutes. Transfer the baking tray to the floor of the roasting oven to crisp the base of the pastry for 5 minutes. Serve hot.

Serves 8.

PORK AND PRUNE CASSEROLE

Prunes go very well with pork and this casserole combines the flavours so well. The pork fillet takes little cooking but the prunes will need soaking in advance.

2 lb/1kg pork fillet
8 oz/225g dried prunes
2 onions, peeled and sliced
seasoned flour
5 fl oz/150ml chicken stock
$^{1}/_{2}$ pint/300ml dry white wine
2 oz/50g butter
1 oz/25g flour

Place the prunes in a bowl and cover with boiling water. Place a plate on top as a lid and leave to stand for at least 4 hours or overnight. Slice the pork fillet into approximately $^{1}/_{2}$"/1.5cm slices. Toss well in the seasoned flour. Melt the butter in a frying pan. Brown the floured meat on all sides. Remove from the heat and keep warm in the simmering oven. Add the onions to the pan and cook over a gentle heat until softened but not brown. Place the onions in an oven-proof dish, then put in the meat.

In the frying pan, make a sauce. Stir the flour into the remaining fat, cook for 1-2 minutes. Gradually stir in the stock, wine and about $\frac{1}{4}$ pint/150ml liquid from the soaking prunes. Season to taste. When boiling, pour over the meat, add the drained prunes and cover.

Cook with the oven shelf on the floor of the roasting oven for 40-50 minutes until the meat is tender and the prunes plumped up. Check the seasoning.

Serves 6.

CARBONNADE OF BEEF

A perfect recipe to make for a crowd. This recipe serves 6, but it is easy to increase the quantities for lots more. Serve a slice of toasted French bread spread with mustard for each portion, to add crunch.

1 clove garlic, peeled and crushed
4 large onions, peeled and sliced
2 oz/50g butter
1 tbsp olive oil
2$\frac{1}{2}$ lb/1.25kg stewing beef, trimmed and cut into cubes
1 good tbsp flour
$\frac{1}{2}$ pint/300ml brown ale
$\frac{1}{2}$ pint/300ml water or beef stock
1 tbsp brown sugar
1 tsp vinegar
salt and pepper
$\frac{1}{2}$ stick French bread
French mustard

Melt half the butter in a frying pan and fry the onions until soft and pale golden brown. Put the onions in a casserole dish. Heat the remaining butter and the oil in the frying pan and brown the meat well. Do this in batches and put on top of onions as the meat is browned. With the last

batch of meat, add the crushed garlic. Sprinkle the flour into the pan juices and cook for 1 minute, stirring well. Gradually add the ale, pour over the meat along with the stock or water, sugar, vinegar, salt and pepper. Cover with a lid. If the casserole dish is flameproof bring to the boil on the simmering plate, alternatively, put it in the roasting oven until bubbling hot. Then transfer to the simmering oven and cook for $2\frac{1}{2}$-3 hours.

About a quarter of an hour before serving, slice the French stick. Lay the bread out on a baking tray and put in the roasting oven with the shelf on the second set of runners from the top. Toast the bread until golden. Turn over and do the second side, then spread it with mustard. Pop it in the oven to heat through and serve with the casserole to mop up the juices.

Serves 6.

PUDDINGS

....

FRUIT BRÛLÉES

....

Brûlées can be difficult to make at home and especially with an Aga, with no grill to caramelise the sugar on top. However, I think you will find this method satisfactory. Make these brûlées in ramekin dishes or cups and serve on saucers.

14oz/400g can pitted cherries or other soft fruit
1 tbsp kirsch
4 egg yolks
2 oz/50g caster sugar
15 fl oz/450ml double cream
6 oz/175g granulated sugar

Drain the cherries and divide between 8 ramekin dishes. Sprinkle over a little kirsch and stand the dishes in the large roasting tin. Fill the kettle and put on to boil. In a mixing bowl whisk together the caster sugar and egg yolks until light and fluffy. Whisk in the cream. Pour the cream mixture over the cherries. Slide the roasting tin half way into the simmering oven and pour round boiling water from the kettle to come about halfway up the ramekins. Gently cook the brûlées for 1 hour. Remove from the oven – they may still be a little wobbly in the middle – and allow to cool completely.

Put the granulated sugar in a heavy based saucepan and heat gently on the simmering plate without stirring for 5-10 minutes until golden brown. Pour a layer of caramel over each cold brûlée. Allow to set for at least one hour, but no more than 6 hours unless sealed with cling film. Serve with a sprig of mint. Suggest to your guests that they crack the caramel with the back of their teaspoon before starting.

....
Serves 8.
....

STRAWBERRIES AND MERINGUE

The combination of a meringue nest filled with strawberries and cream is the epitome of summer. The addition of ground hazelnuts adds texture and flavour. The nuts can be left out if you prefer a clear white meringue or simpler flavour.

3 egg whites
6 oz/175g caster sugar
1 tsp white wine vinegar and 1 tsp cornflour blended
2 oz/50g toasted hazelnuts, ground
¹/₂ pint/300ml double or whipping cream
8 oz/225g fresh strawberries

Line the cold shelf with Bake-O-Glide or non-stick baking parchment. Whisk the egg whites in a clean, dry and grease-free bowl until white and fluffy. Continue to whisk while adding the sugar, 1 teaspoon at a time. Adding the sugar too quickly will cause the meringue to leak. Lightly fold in the cornflour mixture. Gently fold in the ground hazelnuts. Spoon the meringue mix onto the prepared baking sheet. At this point remember the size of plate or tray you are serving the finished dish on! To make a 'basket' spoon the meringue round the sides of the circle.

Bake in the simmering oven for 2 hours until well set. Remove from the baking sheet and turn upside down onto the sheet. Return to the oven, leaving the door slightly ajar, unless your oven is very cool. Continue to dry for 4-6 hours. Remove from the oven and allow to cool before wrapping and storing or filling. When ready to fill, whip the cream until it forms soft peaks. Chop half the strawberries and fold into the cream. Pile the mixture into the meringue shell. Decorate with strawberry halves. Because this method dries out the meringue shell, the meringues can be filled 1-1¹/₂ hours before eating.

Serves 6.

GÂTEAU AU CHOCOLAT

I have served this for a quickly made pudding. Serve with home-made ice-cream or good cream. It is very rich.

4 oz/100g good quality cooking chocolate
4 oz/100g caster sugar
2 tbsp flour
3 eggs, separated
3 oz/75g butter

Butter an 8"/20cm round cake tin. Melt the chocolate by either putting it in a basin on top of the Aga or by placing the basin in the simmering oven. When melted, mix in the softened butter, flour, sugar and beaten egg yolks. Whisk the egg whites until stiff. Gently fold into the chocolate mixture. Turn into the prepared tin. For the two-oven Aga put the oven shelf on the floor of the roasting oven. Put in the cake. Slide the cold shelf onto the second set of runners from the bottom. For the four-oven Aga put the oven shelf on the bottom set of runners in the baking oven. Put in the cake. Bake for 25-30 minutes until there is a crust on the top and the cake is firm to the touch. Cool until it is easy to handle. Turn onto a rack to cool completely. Serve as a cake or pudding with cream and/or fruit.

BRANDY SNAPS

Brandy snap mixture can be moulded over the outsides of oiled ramekins and made into baskets for fresh fruit and cream or rolled around wooden spoon handles for tubes or left flat for fine biscuits to go with home-made ice-cream.

2 oz/50g plain flour
$1/_2$ level tsp ground ginger
2 oz/50g soft brown sugar
1 good tbsp golden syrup
2 oz/50g butter
little grated lemon rind
1 tsp lemon juice

Sieve the flour and ginger onto a plate. Put the remaining ingredients into a saucepan. Heat gently until all is blended. Tip the flour mixture into the saucepan and blend well. Line the cold plain shelf with Bake-O-Glide or parchment. Place 6-8 brandy snaps on the tray – no more than 1 scant teaspoonful each. Slide tray onto the bottom set of runners of the roasting oven. Bake for 5 minutes until golden brown. WATCH as they burn easily. Remove from the heat, allow to crisp for 1-2 minutes and shape – either roll round the greased handles of wooden spoons or drape over greased ramekin dishes to make baskets. Cool. Continue to use all the mixture.

Makes about 20.

FRUIT FLAN

This fruit flan has a smooth, creamy filling. Chill well before topping with fruit and glazing.

8 oz/225g sweet shortcrust pastry
2 oz/50g shelled hazelnuts
2 whole eggs and 2 egg yolks
7 fl oz/200ml crème fraîche
5 fl oz/150ml single cream
3 tbsp icing sugar
selection of seasonal fruits
redcurrant jelly to glaze

Use the pastry to line a 9"/22cm loose-based flan tin. Chill. Put the hazelnuts on a baking tray and toast for 2-3 minutes at the top of the roasting oven. Grind in a processor. Whisk together the nuts, eggs, egg yolks, crème fraîche, single cream and icing sugar. Pour into the pastry case. Bake on the floor of the roasting oven with the cold shelf on the second set of runners from the bottom. Bake for about 30 minutes until the filling is just set and the pastry case golden brown. Cool. Remove the flan ring and stand the flan on a serving plate. Decorate with seasonal fruit. Stand the redcurrant jelly and 1 tablespoon water either on the Aga or in the simmering oven. When melted, use to glaze the flan.

BAKED STRAWBERRY CHEESECAKE

Although this is a baked cheesecake it is light in texture and not too sweet. The layer of fresh strawberries in the base looks attractive when the cheesecake is sliced.

3 oz/75g self-raising flour
1 oz/25g cornflour
3 oz/75g butter
milk for mixing
8 oz/225g fresh strawberries
8 oz/225g cream cheese or mascarpone
2 oz/50g caster sugar
2 eggs, separated
5 fl oz/150ml soured cream

Put the flour and cornflour in a bowl. Add the butter and rub in to resemble breadcrumbs, add a little milk to mix and bind the dough. Roll out onto a lightly floured work surface to a 9"/23cm circle and place in the base of a 9"/23cm spring-release or loose-bottomed cake tin. Arrange three-quarters of the strawberries, sliced over the base mixture. Blend together the cheese, caster sugar, egg yolks and soured cream. Whisk the egg whites until stiff and gently fold into the cheese mixture. Gently pour into the prepared tin, over the strawberries. Stand the cheesecake directly on the flour of the roasting oven and bake for 10 minutes. Then for the two-oven Aga, place the oven shelf on the floor of the roasting oven, put on the cheesecake and then the cold shelf on the second set of runners from the bottom. For the four-oven Aga, transfer to the baking oven. Have the oven shelf on the bottom set of runners. Bake for a further 30-40 minutes until set. Cool and serve warm or cold, decorated with the remaining strawberries, sliced and dusted with icing sugar.

Serves 8.

CHOCOLATE AND ALMOND MERINGUES

....

These meringues can be served as cakes sandwiched together with whipped cream, or make them into small nests and serve them with cream and chocolate sauce for a delicious pudding!

4 egg whites
8 oz/225g caster sugar
2 oz/50g ground almonds
2 oz/50g grated plain chocolate

Weigh out the sugar and have it ready on a plate. Grate the chocolate and mix with the almonds. Line the cold shelf with non-stick parchment or Bake-o-Glide. Whisk the egg whites until white and stiff. Continue whisking while adding the sugar, one teaspoonful at a time. Remove the whisk and gently fold in, with a metal spoon, the chocolate and almond mixture. Make mounds of meringues on the prepared shelf, either 16 halves or 8 nests. Slide onto the third set of runners from the top of the simmering oven and leave to dry out for 2-4 hours, depending upon the warmth of your oven. When cold, fill with whipped cream.

....
Serves 8.
....

TORTA TIRAMISU

This rich, luxurious pudding is perfect for a dinner party. It needs to be made in advance so that it can firm up for slicing. The first time I tasted this it was made with cream, which is very rich. I now use yoghurt instead, but you may prefer to use ¼ pint/150ml whipped double cream.

3 oz/75g butter
4 oz/100g macaroon biscuits e.g. Amaretti
2 x 9 oz/275g tubs mascarpone
4 tbsp strong black coffee
2 oz/50g caster sugar
8 oz/225g plain chocolate
8 oz/225g Greek-style plain yoghurt
2 tbsp icing sugar

Put the butter and the broken chocolate into separate basins and stand them on the Aga to melt. Base line an 8"/20cm loose-bottomed deep cake tin. It will need to be at least 2"/5cm deep. Crush the biscuits and mix in with the melted butter. Press the mixture onto the base of the prepared tin and cool in the fridge while preparing the filling. Beat together one and a half tubs of mascarpone, the caster sugar and the coffee. Beat in the melted chocolate and gently fold in the yoghurt. Pour over the crumb base, level the top and chill for several hours until firm. Beat together the remaining mascarpone and the sieved icing sugar. Spread over the top of the torta. Remove from the tin and serve.

Serves 8-10.

WEEKEND ENTERTAINING

It is fun having family and friends to stay at weekends, but with all those meals to prepare, some pre-cooking will help you cope. Some of the dishes in this section are plainer than the section before, but are more suitable for lunchtime eating and more informal entertaining, and most can be prepared in advance, leaving you time with your guests.

CHICKEN AND APRICOT RAISED PIE

Raised pies are easy to make and look and taste good either for a cold buffet table, a picnic or for a weekend lunch. Make them the day before serving. For this quantity I used an 8"/20cm loose-bottomed sandwich tin, about 1½"/4cm deep. A smaller, deeper tin with a loose bottom helps to remove the pie!

PASTRY:
12 oz/350g plain flour
1 tsp salt
4 oz/100g lard
3 fl oz/75ml water and milk mixed

FILLING:
1 lb/450g skinless, boneless chicken breasts or thighs
4 oz/100g dried apricots
salt and pepper
1 beaten egg to glaze
1 tsp powdered gelatine
5 fl oz/150ml chicken stock

Prepare the hot water crust pastry. Sieve the flour and salt together in a large bowl. In a saucepan, warm the milk, water and lard together until the lard has melted. Place on the boiling plate and bring rapidly to the boil. Pour immediately into the flour. Using a wooden spoon, stir the paste well until a ball of dough is formed and the bowl is left clean. Place on a floured work surface and knead until smooth and elastic. Take two-thirds of the pastry and use this to mould and flatten over the base and sides of the well-greased tin. Mould the paste from the centre to the edge and up the sides using your knuckles. Try not to have too much paste between the base and the sides. Raise sufficiently just to overlap the top of the tin.

Slice the chicken and place half over the base of the pastry case. Season. Lay the apricots on top. Finish with the remaining chicken. Roll the remaining paste out to make a circle to fit the tin. Damp the edges and cover with the lid. Trim and decorate the edges, join well. Make a hole in the centre and decorate with any pastry trimmings. Brush with beaten egg. Stand it on a baking tray. Bake for 20 minutes in the roasting oven with the shelf on the third set of runners from the top. For the two-oven Aga move the oven shelf to the floor of the roasting oven. Put in the pie, slide the cold shelf two runners above the top of the tin. For the four-oven Aga put the oven shelf on the second set of runners from the bottom, transfer the pie. Bake for 2-2$^1/_2$ hours. Brush occasionally with more beaten egg mixture to glaze the top. If it is over-browning lay a sheet of foil over the top.

Remove from the oven and allow to cool before removing from the tin. For the jelly – heat the stock in a small saucepan. Sprinkle in the gelatine and stir until dissolved. Allow to cool until just setting. Using a funnel pour the jelly into the pie through the central hole in the lid. Leave in a cool place to set, preferably overnight.

Serves 6-8.

FARMHOUSE PIE

Farmhouse pie travels well, so it is useful for picnics or for weekend lunches. The pastry is an attractive bright tomato colour.

PASTRY:
8 oz/225g plain flour
pinch salt
4 oz/100g butter
2 tbsp water
1 tbsp tomato purée
1 scant tsp dried oregano

FILLING:
1 lb/450g minced beef
4 sticks celery, chopped
4 spring onions, chopped
2 cloves garlic, peeled and crushed
1 tbsp olive oil
4 oz/100g grated Gruyère or mature Cheddar
3 eggs
1/2 pint/300ml milk
salt and pepper
8"/20cm loose-bottomed cake tin

Sieve the flour and salt together in a mixing bowl. Place the butter, water, tomato purée and oregano together in a small saucepan. Stand the pan on the simmering plate and allow the butter to melt. Bring to the boil and immediately pour into the flour. Stir well until a firm dough forms. Allow to cool slightly. Place the dough in the centre of the tin and use your hand to mould the dough along the base and up the sides of the tin. Crimp the edges. Chill while preparing the filling.

Heat the oil in a medium saucepan, fry the meat until brown and broken up – this is best done rapidly on the boiling plate. Transfer pan to the simmering plate and stir in the celery and onions. Season well. Allow to cook gently for 5 minutes and then tip the meat mixture into the pre-

pared pastry case. Beat together the eggs and milk, and season. Pour the egg mixture gently over the meat mixture – most of this will sink into the meat. Place directly on the floor of the roasting oven and bake for 40 minutes. Remove the sides of the tin, sprinkle the grated cheese over the top and return to the oven for a further 10 minutes until the pastry is crisp and the top golden brown. Serve hot or warm.

Serves 6.

ROAST VEGETABLE LASAGNE

Lasagne seems to be ever popular and is useful to prepare ahead. Choose either fresh pasta sheets or 'no pre-cooking' lasagne. The roasting of the vegetables not only cooks them but brings out a delicious sweetness.

1 1/2 lb/675g selection vegetables e.g. onions, peppers,
aubergines, garlic, courgettes, tomatoes
2 tbsp olive oil
12 oz/350g dried lasagne
8 oz/225g Feta cheese
salt and pepper
1/2 pint/300ml single cream
2 tbsp flour
3 oz/75g grated Sbrinz or Parmesan cheese

Prepare the vegetables. Peel the onions and cut into quarters. Peel the garlic cloves and leave whole. Quarter the tomatoes, dice the aubergines, slice peppers and courgettes. Place in the small roasting tin, drizzle with oil and season with salt. Hang the roasting tin on the top set of runners of the roasting oven and roast for 20-30 minutes, turning occasionally to keep coated in oil. Cook until the vegetables are tender but still keep their

shape. Stir the cream into the flour and season with salt and pepper. Butter an oven-proof dish, preferably a suitable square or oblong shape for the lasagne. Pour enough cream sauce into the base to cover the dish with a thin layer.

Cover the base with a layer of lasagne. Lay half the roast vegetables on top. Dice the Feta cheese and sprinkle half over the vegetables. Lay on another layer of lasagne, add the remaining vegetables and Feta cheese. Cover with another layer of lasagne. Pour over the remaining cream sauce. Scatter on the grated cheese. Put the oven shelf on the bottom set of runners of the roasting oven. Put in the lasagne and bake for 30 minutes. If it is browning too much, cover loosely with foil. This can be kept warm in the simmering oven for half an hour.

Serves 6.

TOMATO AND FETA PIZZAS

Home-made pizzas are delicious for picnics and weekend entertaining. Here I have suggested tomatoes and Feta cheese, but naturally you can ring the changes.

BASE:
12 oz/350g bread flour
1/2 tsp salt
1 sachet easy-blend yeast
2 tbsp olive oil

TOPPING:
4-6 tomatoes
salt and pepper
fresh herbs, basil or rosemary

8-10 black olives, pitted and halved
finely crushed or chopped garlic – 2 or 3 cloves according
to taste
3-4 oz/75-100g Feta cheese, crumbled
3 oz/75g Mozzarella, grated
olive oil

Prepare the pizza dough. Place the flour, salt and yeast in a mixing bowl and stir. Mix in the olive oil. Use hand-warm water to make a firm dough; you will need about ³/₄ pint/450ml, but this depends upon the flour you are using. Knead the dough on a floured work top until it is smooth and stretchy. Roll to a large circle, about 10"/25cm diameter. Brush with olive oil and place oil side down on the cold shelf. Chop the tomatoes thoroughly, place in a basin with the salt, pepper and garlic. Toss well and spread over the pizza base to within ¹/₂"/1cm of the edge. Sprinkle over chopped rosemary or a few torn basil leaves. Crumble over the Feta cheese and the olives. Sprinkle over the grated Mozzarella and drizzle over some olive oil. Slide the pizza onto the second runner from the top of the roasting oven for 15-20 minutes, until the base is crisp and the top is bubbling.

Serves 6-8.

WALNUT BREAD

....

A tasty bread to eat with cheese. The texture will be fairly close due to the weight of the nuts and the wholemeal flour. Serve with good butter and cheese. Add a handful of sultanas to ring the changes.

1 lb/450g wholemeal flour
8 oz/225g strong white flour
1 tsp salt
1 oz/25g fresh yeast
1 tsp sugar
2 tbsp cooking oil
6 oz/175g roughly chopped walnuts
1 pint/600ml warm water

Blend the yeast and sugar together. Add a little water and stand the bowl on top of the Aga until the yeast is frothing. Meanwhile, mix together the flours, salt and nuts in a large bowl or food processor. Add the yeast mixture and most of the water. Mix well to make a smooth dough, adding more water as necessary. Knead the dough on a floured work top for 5 minutes or for 20-30 seconds in the food processor. Return the dough to the mixing bowl, cover lightly with a clean tea towel and stand on a trivet on top of the simmering plate lid until the dough has doubled in size.

Knock back the dough on a floured work top. Divide the mixture in two. Shape each half into a loaf and place on a well-greased and floured baking tray. Cover again with the tea towel and return to the trivet on top of the simmering plate lid. Leave until doubled in size. Place the oven shelf on the third set of runners from the top of the roasting oven. Slide in the bread and bake for 30-35 minutes until it is golden brown, comes out of the tin easily and sounds hollow when tapped on the bottom. Cool on a wire rack.

Makes 2 loaves.
....

CHEAT'S ONION BREAD

This makes a good bread for picnics and weekend lunches. It is quick to make, especially if you have the use of a food processor.

12 oz/350g strong plain flour
1 sachet easy-blend yeast
1/2 tsp salt
1 tbsp vegetable oil
1/2 packet onion soup mix
1/2 pint/300ml warm water
egg for glazing – optional

Measure the flour, yeast, salt and soup mix into a food processor or mixing bowl. Add the oil and enough warm water to make a dough. Remove from the bowl and knead until smooth and stretchy. Grease and flour a 1 1/2 lb/700g loaf tin. Put in the bread dough. Stand the tin on top of a folded tea towel or mat on top of the simmering plate, cover with a clean tea towel until doubled in size. Brush with egg if using. Put the oven shelf on the bottom set of runners of the roasting oven, put in the bread and bake for 30-40 minutes until risen, golden brown and sounds hollow when tapped on the bottom. Cool on a wire rack.

Makes 1 medium-sized loaf.

PECAN TARTS

I find the combination of chocolate and nuts irresistible. Pecans have a distinctive flavour and texture and are expensive, so walnuts can be substituted. This recipe will make one large 9"/22.5cm pie or six individual tarts. I use muffin tins which give deep tarts with plenty of filling; this quantity will make 12.

6 oz/175g plain white flour
4 oz/100g butter
1 oz/25g icing sugar
1 egg yolk
6 oz/175g plain chocolate
2 oz/50g butter
4 eggs
6 oz/175g maple syrup
a few drops vanilla essence
8 oz/225g shelled pecan nuts
icing sugar

Sieve the icing sugar and flour together into a large bowl. Cut the butter into cubes and rub into the flour until the mixture resembles fine breadcrumbs. Bind with the beaten egg yolk and enough water to make a firm, smooth dough. Wrap and chill. When the pastry is chilled roll out to fit either a 9"/22.5cm tart tin or 12 muffin tins. Chill again. Put the broken chocolate and butter in a basin and stand in a warm spot on the Aga until melted. Whisk together the eggs, maple syrup and vanilla essence. Whisk in the chocolate mixture. Reserve 12 whole pecans. Roughly chop the remaining nuts and stir into the egg mixture. Pour into the pastry cases and top with the whole pecans. Bake, standing the tins directly on the floor of the roasting oven, 20 minutes for the small tarts and 30 minutes for the large tart, or until just set in the middle and the pastry is golden around the edges. Serve warm or cold dusted with icing sugar.

Serves 8-12.

PLUM TATIN

....

Plums are delicious in Autumn and are useful for all sorts of desserts. This makes an attractive dessert both for Saturday lunches or even for supper parties. The plums can of course be interchanged with apples.

1 lb/450g plums
butter to grease dish
2 tbsp soft brown sugar
6 oz/175g plain flour
pinch salt
3 oz/75g butter
2 egg yolks
1 tbsp caster sugar

Butter the sides and base of 8"-10"/20-25cm oven-proof dish or cake tin (not loose-bottomed!) Sprinkle the brown sugar over the base of the tin. Cut the plums in half and remove the stones. Lay them on the base of the prepared tin, cut side up. Set aside. Prepare the pastry. Sieve the flour and salt together in a bowl, stir in the sugar. Rub in the butter until the mixture resembles fine breadcrumbs. Bind the mixture together with the egg yolks. Use some cold water to bind the mixture if needed. Roll to a circle slightly larger than the dish used for the plums. Moisten the edge of the circle and fold over the excess pastry to form a ridge. Turn pastry over and place it on top of the plums. Press down lightly. If time allows, chill for half an hour to allow the pastry to rest.

Bake directly on the floor of the roasting oven for 30-40 minutes until the fruit is bubbling around the sides. Allow to sit for 5 minutes before turning out onto a plate, plum sides uppermost. The plums should be glazed with the sugar syrup. Serve warm or cold.

Makes 6-8 slices.
....

APPLE CAKE

Apple cake can be served warm as a pudding or cold as a cake. It travels well, so is useful for picnics or as a pudding for informal entertaining.

1 1/2 lb/675g eating apples
butter for greasing
2 tbsp soft brown sugar
3 eggs
6 oz/175g self-raising flour
6 oz/175g soft brown sugar
6 oz /175g soft margarine

Butter a 10"/25cm cake tin or oven-proof dish. Sprinkle the 2 table-spoons sugar over the base. Quarter, core and slice half the apples and lay decoratively over the base of the prepared tin. Peel, quarter, core and chop the remaining apples. Place in a mixing bowl, add the eggs, flour, sugar and margarine. Beat well until the mixture is smooth. Gently spoon over the apples. Level the top. Stand the tin directly on the floor of the roasting oven, slide the cold shelf onto the second set of runners from the bottom. Bake for about 30 minutes until the sponge is risen and golden. Test the middle with a skewer to see that the mixture is cooked, some apples are very moist. To serve, turn out onto a plate so that the caramelised apples are on the top.

Serves 8.

JANE'S TEABREAD

We have often had this for tea at the house of our friends Jane and Tom. I usually make two or three for fêtes and bazaars, as it is easy to make and bake. Serve sliced and buttered.

10 oz/275g mixed dried fruit
6 oz/175g soft brown sugar
$1/_2$ pint/300ml tea
10 oz/275g self-raising flour
1 egg

In a mixing bowl mix together the dried fruits and sugar. Pour on the tea, cover and allow to stand for 4-5 hours or overnight. After soaking, beat in the flour and beaten egg. Stir to mix well. Grease a 2lb/1kg loaf tin well and line the base with greaseproof paper. Put in the cake mixture and level the top. For the two-oven Aga, put the oven shelf on the floor of the roasting oven. Place in the cake and bake for 15 minutes. After 15 minutes slide in the cold shelf, allowing room for the teabread to rise. Bake for a further 45 minutes. For the four-oven Aga, put the shelf on the bottom set of runners and bake for 45 minutes until risen, golden brown and cooked in the middle when tested with a skewer.

HAZELNUT SHORTBREAD

....

Thick slices of hazelnut shortbread with fresh fruit and tea make a good pudding for weekend entertaining. It is ideal for Saturday lunchtime, and can be made a day or two in advance.

12 oz/350g plain flour
8 oz/225g butter
4 oz/100g caster sugar
2 oz/50g ground hazelnuts

This makes two rounds which fit onto the cold shelf. Line the shelf with baking parchment or Bake-O-Glide. Sieve the flour in a mixing bowl. Add the butter and rub in to resemble breadcrumbs. Stir in the sugar and ground nuts. Now work the mixture with your hand to bind together to make a smooth dough. When ready, cut the mixture in half. Pat out 2 rounds on the prepared cold shelf. Pinch the edges to decorate and prick all over with a fork.

For a two-oven Aga, slide the shelf onto the bottom set of runners of the roasting oven. Check for browning after 10 minutes and turn the shelf round if necessary. Bake for 20 minutes. For a four-oven Aga, slide the shelf onto the bottom set of runners of the baking oven and bake for 30 minutes. Remove from the oven and slice each into 8 portions. Cool on a wire rack and dust with caster sugar.

....
Makes 16.
....

THAI MEAL

As Thai restaurants have proliferated around Britain so Thai style cooking has become increasingly popular. The mix of flavours appeals to us and once the preparations are complete, the cooking is often quick. I have tried to adapt this Thai menu so that not too many unusual ingredients are needed, and everything can be bought in a supermarket.

This menu can be prepared in advance, and although I give ingredients for four, I have chosen this menu because it can easily be adapted for larger numbers.

PRAWN BASKETS

Prepare the filo baskets well ahead of time, they can be a little fiddly to make. I usually make one or two extra in case they break – they tend to be fragile but look so effective.

BASKETS:
4 sheets filo pastry
sunflower oil

PRAWN FILLING:
8 oz/225g prawns
2 tbsp sunflower oil
1 bunch spring onions
2 cloves garlic, peeled
1 small red chilli, seeded
4 oz/100g button mushrooms
2 oz/50g mangetout peas
1 tbsp coriander, chopped
grated rind of $1/2$ lemon
pinch salt
pinch sugar
1 tbsp soy sauce

Prepare the baskets. You will need 4 ramekin dishes standing on a baking sheet. Cut the filo pastry into 4 squares – it may need trimming, depending on the size of your filo sheets. Brush one square of pastry with oil. Lay this, oil side down, over the base and sides of an upturned ramekin dish. Oil the next sheet of pastry and lay over the first sheet, slightly turning do that the points of the square come to a different position. This makes the basket look more attractive. Continue so that each ramekin is covered with 4 sheets of filo pastry. Bake on the third set of runners from the top in the roasting tin for 12-15 minutes until golden and crispy. Allow to cool completely before removing each basket from its mould.

Prepare the filling. This can be served warm or cold. Cut the green ends from two spring onions and cut them into shreds, set aside in cold water to garnish. Rinse the prawns and remove the intestines if using tiger prawns. Finely slice the remaining onions, garlic and chilli. Finely slice the mushrooms, trim the mangetout and cut them in half. Heat the sunflower oil in a large frying pan or wok on the boiling plate. Add the onions, garlic, and chilli and stir well for 2-3 minutes. Add the mushrooms. Stir well for 30 seconds then add the mangetout and prawns. Continue stir-frying for 2-3 minutes. Add the remaining ingredients, move to the simmering plate for 2-3 minutes. Spoon into the filo baskets when ready to serve. Garnish with onion shreds.

Serves 4.

GRILLED THAI CHICKEN

Serve this chicken hot from the oven with fragrant Thai rice, or cold with a salad. If serving cold, the chicken is best sliced after cooking. Marinate overnight for a full flavour. Shallot chutney is a good accompaniment whether hot or cold.

4 chicken breasts or quarters

MARINADE:
1 tbsp sunflower oil
2 tsp sesame oil
2 thin red chillies, seeded and chopped
2 cloves garlic, peeled and crushed
1 tsp cumin seeds
1 tsp fennel seeds
1 tbsp fresh basil, chopped
1 tsp turmeric
1 tbsp soft brown sugar
2 tbsp tomato purée
salt to taste

Heat the oils together in a small saucepan. Add the chillies, garlic, cumin seeds, fennel seeds, basil and turmeric and fry gently for 4-5 minutes, taking care not to burn. Remove from the heat and stir in the remaining ingredients. Stir well and return to the heat to dissolve the sugar – a thick marinade is formed. Leave to cool. Slash through the chicken skin and into the breast meat. Put the chicken into a non-metal dish and smear the chicken with the marinade. Cover and chill for 8 hours or overnight. Put the grill rack inside the roasting tin and lay the chicken pieces on it. Slide the tin onto the second set of runners in the roasting oven and grill for 15-20 minutes. Turn over and repeat. Serve immediately with fragrant Thai rice, or chill and serve sliced with salads.

Serves 4.

SHALLOT CHUTNEY

Make this a day or two ahead for a full, deep flavour. The sweet-sour flavour goes well with chicken and other spicy foods.

8 oz/225g shallots, peeled
1 clove garlic, peeled and chopped
1 tbsp oil
1 tbsp dry sherry
3 tbsp wine vinegar
2 oz/50g caster sugar
8 oz/225g small tomatoes
2 tbsp sweet soy sauce
3 tbsp water

Heat the oil in a medium-sized pan or casserole with oven-proof handles. Toss the garlic and shallots in the hot oil and transfer the pan to the floor of the roasting oven for 15-20 minutes or until the shallots are golden brown. Add the vinegar, sherry, sugar and water. Stir and return to the floor of the roasting oven for 15 minutes. Halve the tomatoes and stir into the shallot mixture. Cook to soften the tomatoes about 5-10 minutes, depending upon ripeness. Stir and put into a bowl to cool.

THAI FRAGRANT RICE

8 oz/225g Thai rice
15 fl oz/450ml cold water

Put the rice in a sieve and rinse very well under running water. Place the rice in a saucepan. Pour on water. Cover. Stand pan on the boiling plate and bring to the boil. As soon as the rice boils transfer the pan to the simmering oven for 10 minutes. Remove from the oven, fork through, re-cover and stand for 4-5 minutes. Fork through again and serve.

CHINESE MEAL

Chinese food is now very popular and with so much pre-preparation necessary it is easy to prepare a Chinese meal for guests. Eat the Chinese way by making several different dishes and putting them all on the table together so that guests can have a little of everything. The ideas for this menu came about when Aga launched their new wok. If you do not have a wok use a large, deep frying pan for stir-frying.

FIVE SPICE LAMB

Lamb cubed from a leg joint will cook in one hour, but some tougher cuts may take $1^{1}/_{2}$-2 hours. This is an easy casserole.

1$^{1}/_{2}$ lb/675g lamb, cubed
3 cloves garlic, crushed
1 tsp root ginger, finely chopped
1 tsp five spice powder
5 tbsp soy sauce
3 tbsp dry sherry
15 fl oz/450ml beef stock
1$^{1}/_{2}$ oz/35g soft brown sugar
1 tbsp cornflour
fresh coriander leaves for garnish

Mix all the ingredients together, except the cornflour, and leave to marinade for 4 hours or even overnight. Pour into a flameproof casserole, stand it on the boiling plate and bring to the boil Transfer to the simmering oven and cook for 1-2 hours – see note above. Blend the cornflour with some water to make a paste. Just before serving, stir the cornflour into the casserole, allow to boil either in the roasting oven or on the simmering plate until a thick sauce is formed. Garnish with coriander.

Serves 6.

BAMBOO SHOOT PRAWNS

....

12 large prawns
1 stick celery
4 spring onions
4 bamboo shoots
2 tbsp ground nut oil
1 tsp root ginger, finely chopped

Peel the prawns, finely slice the celery, spring onions and bamboo shoots into long, thin strips. Heat the oil in a heavy-based frying pan, either on the simmering plate or on the floor of the roasting oven. Stir in the ginger and cook, stirring for 1-2 minutes. Add the prawns and vegetables and cook, stirring, until the prawns turn pink. Serve immediately.

Serves 6.
....

SPRING ROLLS

These can be made very successfully without deep-frying. You can vary the filling and even use a packet of stir-fry mix for a quick filling. A few small prawns could be added.

1 tbsp vegetable oil
1 red pepper, de-seeded and cut into strips
2 oz/50g mangetout peas, topped and tailed and cut into strips
2 oz/50g bamboo shoots, cut into strips
2 oz/50g beansprouts
2 spring onions, finely sliced
½ tsp salt
1 tsp soy sauce
1 tsp sesame oil
1 tbsp dry sherry
8 sheets filo pastry
4 oz/100g butter

Stand the butter, in a basin, on top of the Aga to allow the butter to melt. In a large frying pan heat the vegetable oil on the boiling plate. Stir in the prepared vegetables and stir-fry for 1-2 minutes. Add the salt, soy sauce, sesame oil and dry sherry. Cook for another minute or two. Put to one side and allow to cool. Line the roasting tin with Bake-O-Glide or non-stick parchment. You will need the large tin if making 16 small rolls, but the small one will do for 8 large rolls. Lay out the filo pastry in a pile. Brush the top sheet with melted butter. If making small rolls cut the sheet in half. Lay on a strip of filling mixture. Roll the pastry round the edges to make a parcel. Lay each roll in the prepared tin. Continue until all the pastry and filling is used up. Brush the rolls with the remaining butter. Slide the roasting tin on the top set of runners of the roasting oven and cook for 20 minutes until golden and crisp all over. Serve immediately.

Makes 8 large or 16 small rolls.

STIR-FRIED LEMON CHICKEN

This recipe has a lovely sharp flavour and looks attractive with the combination of yellow and red. It has been adapted from the Aga wok recipes.

1 1/2 lb/650g boneless chicken breasts
1 tsp salt
ground pepper
5 tbsp vegetable oil
1"/2.5cm piece root ginger, finely chopped
1 red pepper, de-seeded and finely sliced
shredded rind of 2 lemons
6 spring onions, sliced
4 tbsp dry sherry
1 1/2 tsp sugar
2 tbsp soy sauce
1 tsp cornflour
2 tbsp lemon juice

Cut the chicken into bite-sized pieces. Add the vegetable oil, salt and pepper and toss well. Set aside. Mix together sherry, sugar, soy sauce, lemon juice and the cornflour blended with a little water. Heat a wok or large frying pan on the boiling plate. Add all the oil and the chicken and stir briskly for 2-3 minutes. Add the pepper and ginger, stirring all the time. Then add the lemon rind and spring onions followed by the sauce of sherry and lemon juice. Continue stir-frying for 1-2 minutes and serve.

Serves 6.

RICE

Cook the rice in the simmering oven so that the plates are free for stir-frying. White rice is usually served with Chinese-style meals.

3 large cups white rice
5 cups water
1 tsp salt

Place the rice, water and salt in a saucepan. Cover and bring to the boil. Transfer to the simmering oven and allow to cook for 10 minutes. Check the rice: some varieties will be cooked, some may need a further minute or two. Drain and rinse rice with boiling water. Serve in a warm dish, or if not quite ready, cover and keep hot in the simmering oven.

Serves 6.

VEGETABLES IN OYSTER SAUCE

A variety of vegetables can be used for this dish. Have a mix of colours and textures, the vegetables are only briefly cooked, so they remain bright and the texture crunchy. If you prefer slightly less crunchy vegetables cook for 2-3 minutes longer.

1 lb/450g vegetables e.g. carrots, broccoli, courgettes, mush-
rooms, mangetout peas, baby sweetcorn
2 tbsp vegetable oil
2 cloves garlic, peeled and crushed
pinch salt
2 tbsp dry sherry
1/2 tsp sugar
2-3 tbsp oyster sauce

Prepare the vegetables. Cut to an even size, not too large. Any hard or older vegetables e.g. carrots and broccoli should be blanched in boiling water for 1-2 minutes to help the cooking. Heat the oil in a large saucepan. Add the garlic, sherry, salt, pepper and sugar and stir. While stirring, add the vegetables. Cover and cook for 1-2 minutes. Drain and place on a serving dish. Pour the oyster sauce over the vegetables.

Serves 6.

EXOTIC FRUIT SALAD

At the end of a Chinese meal, serve a selection of fruit or an exotic fruit salad. The Chinese rarely eat puddings as we know them, and you may find them too filling anyway. Serve almond biscuits or brandy snaps to go with it.

4 oz/100g white sugar
$^1/_2$ pint/300ml water
pared rind and juice of 1 lemon
a selection of fruits e.g. pineapple, star fruit, satsumas,
strawberries, lychees, kumquats

Choose a selection of fruits available in season. Consider colours, textures and size. Have about 4 different fruits. Place the sugar and water in a saucepan, stand it on the simmering plate and stir while the sugar dissolves. Add the lemon rind and juice and bring to the boil. Remove from the heat and allow to cool. Pour into a serving dish. Prepare the fruit according to type. Toss in the syrup. Chill and serve.

POACHED PEACHES

Poaching of peaches and nectarines brings out their flavour. Other soft fruits can be served with these peaches. Serve with almond biscuits or thick almond shortbread.

6 large peaches
$1/_2$ pint/300ml water
5 fl oz/150ml orange juice
2 oz/50g sugar

Put the water, orange juice and sugar in a saucepan. Stand the pan over a medium heat to dissolve the sugar. Peel, quarter and stone the peaches, and add them to the sugar syrup. Bring to the boil, cover and place in the simmering oven. Poach the fruit. The length of time depends upon the ripeness of the fruit – anything from $1/_4$ to $3/_4$ hour. Remove the fruit to a serving dish, bring the juice to the boil and boil until thickened and syrupy. Pour over the fruit. Serve warm or chilled.

Serves 6.

ALMOND BISCUITS

These biscuits are like macaroons in appearance and texture. The almonds on the top can be changed for walnuts or cherries.

4 oz/100g self-raising flour
1 tsp baking powder
1¹/₂ oz/35g lard
4 oz/100g caster sugar
2 eggs, beaten
16-20 almonds, walnut halves or cherry halves

Sieve the flour and baking powder into a bowl. Rub in the lard to make a fine breadcrumb mixture. Add the beaten eggs to make a soft mixture. Line the cold shelf with non-stick parchment or Bake-O-Glide. Space out teaspoonfuls of mixture, about 12 to a tray. Top each with a cherry or nut. Bake on the bottom set of runners of the roasting oven for about 8-10 minutes until risen and pale golden in colour. These can also be baked on the third set of runners in the baking oven of a four-oven Aga for 12-15 minutes. Cool on a wire rack.

Makes 16-18 biscuits.

INDEX

ACKNOWLEDGEMENTS

Thank you to all the people who have helped with the book; not just the practical hands on help but with inspiration. As a reader of recipes and cookery articles for as long as I can remember, many previous writers have inspired me. My mother was a fan of Katie Stewart and I have used and adapted her common-sense recipes since school days. I must thank Kym Holroyd at the Aga Shop, Bath, for all her encouragement, Jon Croft of Absolute Press for his confidence, but especially my editor Bronwen Douglas who has kept me on the straight and narrow when the going got tough. Also Ann Coleborn for making sense of my handwriting and keeping me to deadline. The recipes have all been tested by me on my faithful 2 oven Aga. A select band of friends have nobly sampled many of the dishes, and the Christmas cakes have been tasted and tested by the boys of Westminster Cathedral Choir, their housemasters and matron. The remaining recipes have been tried and tested by my children Hanna, Dominic and Hugo and my long-suffering husband Geoff. Thank you to everyone.